Measuring and Improving
Employee Motivation

Measuring and Improving Employee Motivation

PETER FARGUS

FINANCIAL TIMES

Prentice Hall

An imprint of Pearson Education

London	New York	San Francisco	Toronto	Sydney
Tokyo	Singapore	Hong Kong	Cape Town	Madrid
Paris	Milan	Munich	Amsterdam	

PEARSON EDUCATION LIMITED

Head Office:
Edinburgh Gate
Harlow CM20 2JE
Tel: +44 (0)1279 623623
Fax: +44 (0)1279 431059

London Office:
128 Long Acre
London WC2E 9AN
Tel: +44 (0)20 7447 2000
Fax: +44 (0)20 7240 5771
Website: www.business-minds.com

First published in Great Britain in 2000

© Peter Fargus 2000

The right of Peter Fargus to be identified as author
of this work has been asserted by him in accordance
with the Copyright, Designs and Patents Act 1988.

ISBN 0 273 65006 8

British Library Cataloguing in Publication Data
A CIP catalogue record for this book can be obtained from the British Library.

10 9 8 7 6 5 4 3 2 1

Typeset by Boyd Elliott Typesetting
Printed and bound in Great Britain

The Publishers' policy is to use paper manufactured from sustainable forests.

About the author

Peter Fargus is a Chartered Psychologist who trained as a Management Consultant with the Urwick Consulting Group in the 1980s. In addition he has worked for Rowntree Mackintosh in York and Toronto, British Airways at Heathrow and the First National Bank of Chicago in London. Currently he and his wife, Dee, work as a partnership, helping organisations to measure the motivation of their people and implement appropriate improvement action. Past clients range from small family companies to the largest of multinationals.

The Fargus Consulting Partnership can be contacted at

Glenwood Lodge
Beechwood Crescent
Harrogate
North Yorkshire HG2 0PA
England

Tel: 0044 (1) 423 566035
Fax: 0044 (1) 423 531 710
Website: www.fcp-surveys.com
E-mail: fargus@fcp-surveys.com

Contents

Preface

WHO SHOULD READ THIS BOOK?

This book is aimed at senior management teams the members of which feel that they need a systematic way of motivating their employees on a continuous basis. Although the smallest organisation described in this book employs 800 people, the author has used the same principles outlined in organisations with as few as 100 people.

QUICK READ

Executives today are hard pressed for time, and some hints for getting the most out of this book in the shortest time are outlined below. Note that definitions of terms used and abbreviations can be found at the front of the book.

For members of the senior management team

Obtain a flavour of the content by reading the Executive Summary and the key point summaries at the end of each chapter.

If you want to read more, the chapters on which to concentrate are 1–3 and 8–10. Use subheadings for a 'quick read'.

Chapter 1 provides the reasoning behind the use of employee surveys.

For human resource executives

Normally it is you who are tasked with designing and implementing a survey. If this is so, you are advised to read everything. But you too are likely to be short of time. You will find that all chapters have subheadings to facilitate a quick read.

The following quotes capture the essence of the whole book:

> *The best way to work out how to improve your business is to ask your people. Who else is in better touch with the realities?*
>
> Keith Weed, Chairman, Elida Fabergé.

Financial managers rely on regular reports to monitor the financial health of their business. What do people managers have? Historically very little. But if 'people are our most important asset' shouldn't there be a regular way of monitoring the health of the human side of the business?

Clive Newton, Senior Partner – PricewaterhouseCoopers

Acknowledgements

Airtours Holidays: Janice Timberlake, Human Resources Director, and Beverley Seddon, Personnel Manager, for their contributions.

AS Imada and Associates: Andy Imada, for allowing the results of his interventions to be included.

British Quality Foundation: for permitting the use of the European Foundation for Quality Management 1998 Business Excellence Model.

BT Multi-National Sales and Service: Joe McDavid, Human Resources Manager, and Sarah Gill, HR Project Manager, for their contributions.

Elida Fabergé: Andrew Shephard, Business Excellence Manager, for his contributions.

FCP team: Dee Fargus, Julie Green, Kandy Harrop for researching, typing and proofreading.

Focus Central London: for allowing the material taken from *Doing Business Better – the long term impact of Investors in People* to be reproduced. Copies can be obtained from Focus Central London, Centre Point, 103 New Oxford Street, London, WC1A 1DR.

Institute for Employment Studies: for allowing the material taken from *From People to Profits* to be reproduced. Copies are available from: IES Mantell Building, Falmer, Brighton BN1 9RF.

Institute of Personnel and Development: for allowing the material taken from the *Impact of People Management Practices on Business Performance* to be reproduced. Copies are available from: IPD House, Camp Road, London SW19 4UX.

Leeds University Statistical Services: Dr Lisa Walder for her advice on the statistical issues.

PricewaterhouseCoopers: Clive Newton, PricewaterhouseCoopers Global Human Resource Leader for enabling the use of PwC examples; Charlie Keeling, Global Human Resources Leader PricewaterhouseCoopers MCS; Scottie Ruane, Jenna Stephens, Global Human Resources Team; Kevin Walker, PricewaterhouseCoopers MCS Survey Centre, for their contributions.

Mercator Computer Systems: Steve Jenkins, Director, for providing up-to-date information on electronic distribution and retrieval.

And to the anonymous contributions by those who, by virtue of their anonymity, cannot be publicly thanked.

Definitions

In this book the following definitions apply:

Airtours	Airtours Holidays Ltd.
BT	British Telecommunications.
Correlation	A measure of the relationship between two ranges of data. A high correlation means there is a strong linear relationship. A weak correlation means there is very little relationship.
Cut	A section of data that describes responses from a subsection of a population of employees, e.g. department, gender, length of service.
Demotivator	Action or situation that diminishes interest in, or ability to meet, organisational goals.
FCP	Fargus Consulting Partnership.
Free format	Written/typed answers to an open question.
Hard measure	A measure based on a count of specific occurrences of number, e.g. days lost through sickness.
Html	Hyper text mark-up language used for creating more professional looking documentation on the Internet.
Instrument	The document designed to establish a soft measure in the form of a questionnaire (term interchangeable with questionnaire).
Leader	PricewaterhouseCoopers' term for a person who is responsible for the planning and monitoring of someone else's work. Managers do not always take this role.
MCS	PricewaterhouseCoopers Management Consultancy Services.
MNS&S	BT Multi-National Sales and Service.
Morale	A feeling of self-esteem – high or low.
Motivation	Interests and abilities harnessed towards meeting team and/or organisational goals.
Motivator	Action or situation which harnesses interest in or ability to meet organisational goals.
PwC	PricewaterhouseCoopers.

Questionnaire	The document which provides a soft measure of motivation (term interchangeable with instrument).
Regression	The linear relationship between two ranges of data where the value from one range enables the prediction of a value from the second range.
Satisfier	Action which may increase morale but does not create sustained motivation, e.g. basic pay which is perceived to be fair.
Senior management team	The most senior managers running an organisation or part of one, for example the board, the executive committee, the divisional executive, etc.
Service Line	An autonomous division of Pricewaterhouse Coopers.
Significant difference	A difference between two sets of figures which is unlikely to have happened by chance.
Soft measure	A measure based on people's perception of actuality, e.g. a person's view on whether senior management act as a team.
TQM	Total Quality Management.

Executive summary

Actively taking steps to harness your people's abilities and interests in order to meet organisational goals has been shown to increase productivity, reduce costs and improve customer satisfaction. For example:

- *The Sheffield Effectiveness Programme* shows that people management practices have by far the highest impact on profitability and productivity compared to any other management practice.

- *The Institute of Employment Studies* research demonstrates that the implementation of Investors in People has a statistically significant impact on productivity and customer satisfaction. They also found that in the retail world an increase in employee commitment led to major increases in sales.

- *The Imada Loss Prevention Programme* which recommended improved people management practices within a division of a multinational oil company, succeeded in significantly reducing lost work days and reduced costs by 30 per cent over a period of ten years.

Although there is hard evidence accumulating that a motivated workforce produces business results, most senior management teams take this as read. They intuitively accept that a key to the competitive edge of their organisation lies in the way their people use their brains – and harnessing this brainpower is becoming one of the major issues in the twenty-first century.

Over the last twenty years, the author has been involved in harnessing abilities and interests in businesses ranging from small family-owned organisations to the largest of multinationals. From an analysis of employee viewpoints solicited over this time, it is clear that common influences on motivation include:

- how senior managers behave;
- how people are managed;
- how efficient the organisation is;
- how resources are managed;
- reputation and success.

In this book divisions of four leading organisations have agreed to demonstrate how they value and measure the motivation of their people.

Airtours Plc is the world's largest provider of air-inclusive holidays. Airtours Holidays Ltd, the largest UK tour operator within the Airtours group of companies, has over 2,000 employees worldwide. The company has been using surveys to help assess employee motivation since 1995.

BT's Multi-National Sales and Service directorate provided communications to major global customers and employed about 2,000 people. (The directorate no longer exists due to reorganisation caused by the launch of BT's Global Venture with AT&T.) The survey referred to in this book supplemented the annual company employee satisfaction survey, feedback from focus groups and monthly capability management surveys. BT itself has been running employee surveys since 1989.

Elida Fabergé is part of Home and Personal Care – Europe, one of 12 business groups within Unilever. The company manufactures and markets personal care products including deodorants and shampoos, employing 600 people in Leeds and 200 in London. The organisation has been carrying out regular employee surveys linked to its drive for continuous improvement since 1991.

PricewaterhouseCoopers (PwC) is one of the world's largest professional services organisations resulting from the merger of Price Waterhouse and Coopers and Lybrand. Management Consultancy Services (MCS) operates in 62 countries and employs 35,000 professional staff and 5,000 support staff. It has been carrying out regular employee surveys since 1987. In addition to explaining how MCS motivates their people, examples from other PricewaterhouseCoopers Service Lines have been used.

The lessons from these four contributors are summarised below.

WHAT GETS MEASURED GETS TREASURED

Pressures today are such that urgent matters take precedence over important matters, and if management's attention is directed away from employee relations, people issues become low priority.

By establishing a meaningful measure of motivation, the senior management team is signalling they value those aspects of management that impact on motivation, and are regularly reminded of those aspects of management that influence motivation.

PUT YOUR MEASUREMENT OF MOTIVATION IN CONTEXT

Your measure of people motivation should be as important as your other performance indicators and should be incorporated into a selection of measures which monitor the execution of your business plan. There are different approaches to doing this, but three powerful ones are:

- the use of the EFQM/BQF model of Business Excellence;
- the creation of a tailor-made performance index;
- the use of a balanced scorecard;

or a combination of the three.

MAKE YOUR MEASURING INSTRUMENT ONE THAT STANDS THE TEST OF TIME

Make it the responsibility of your senior management team to oversee the development of your approach to measuring motivation. Assemble a team of people respected by your organisation to do the legwork and make sure they incorporate both hard and soft measures of the full range of influences on motivation.

Soft measures require the use of an employee opinion survey. Make sure any survey acknowledges the current 'hot issues' to show your people that you are 'in touch'. The finished instrument should be one which can be used regularly without major edits.

INVOLVE ALL YOUR PEOPLE

If it is administratively possible, chose the option of an 'all-organisation' survey because one of your main objectives is to involve your people – make them feel that their voice counts. Your people will value their 'voice at the table'.

Increase the probability of a good response by making sure influential people within your organisation are 'on side', by guaranteeing confidentiality and by advertising that action will be taken.

Once people are used to being consulted using survey technology, or if you need a quick snapshot of current sentiment, you can then go for the 'sample' approach. This provides valid results but does not offer 100 per cent involvement.

ENSURE YOU USE EXPERIENCED PEOPLE TO MAKE THE DATA MEANINGFUL

Capturing data and making it meaningful enough to tease out themes and trends is full of pitfalls for the uninitiated. Make sure the people you use can be trusted to keep individual responses confidential and provide data which itself is trusted by your senior management team.

USE PICTURES TO DEMONSTRATE ISSUES

The old adage about a picture being worth a thousand words is true when it comes to presenting results. The use of standard presentation techniques (spreadsheets, bar charts, pie charts) can highlight both positive and negative influences on motivation without recourse to lengthy written reports. Use more advanced statistical techniques to investigate your data in more detail.

GIVE SPEEDY FEEDBACK TO YOUR PEOPLE

Once you have the results, unless you can reach quick decisions as to the actions you intend to take, do not delay feedback until you have an action plan. Delays are the life blood of the cynic. Provide feedback on results – both overall and on individual departments – quickly and decide on actions to be taken later.

INVOLVE YOUR PEOPLE IN DECIDING ON IMPROVEMENT ACTION

The fact that you are willing to take action has itself a motivating effect on your people. But the act of involving them in recommending what actions should be taken (within defined limits of course) is a major motivator. If done correctly the feedback and involvement can energise your whole organisation.

CONSIDER TRAINING IN PARALLEL WITH ACTION

Some improvement action can be done quickly and relatively easily. Other improvements can be tricky to implement because they require changes in behaviour both from managers and non-managers.

A combination of drip feed communication and focused training is sometimes a necessary prerequisite to sustained improvements. How much, and what training? That depends on the level of competence your people currently have and the actions required as a result of your survey, but can include both management and non-management training.

TAKE ACTION AND BLOW YOUR TRUMPET

Once you have involved people in making recommendations make sure that high-profile action is taken. If decisions are made to take no action – explain why. When action is taken, make sure people associate it with the survey and subsequent discussions. Keep up the drip feed communication and make sure people link the actions taken with the survey results. By doing this you increase the probability of a good response to your next survey.

Typically actions chosen should aim to have an impact on the main influences on motivation. Examples from the contributors include actions aimed at:

- *how senior managers behave* through establishing an organisation-wide value set;
- *how people are managed* through upward feedback and personal development;
- *how efficient the organisation is* by redesigning/streamlining business processes;
- *how resources are managed* by targeted investment in information technology;
- *reputation and success* through improved product definition and delivery.

LINK THE RESULTS TO YOUR BUSINESS PLAN

Do not measure motivation as a separate initiative. If 'people are your most valuable asset' make sure the measures you take are incorporated into your business planning alongside your financial data and customer feedback.

KEEP TABS ON WHAT IS HAPPENING

Make sure you have a system of monitoring what is going on as a result of your survey. You need to do this to measure the levels of improvement action, recognise effort and congratulate successes.

Why measure motivation?

What gets measured gets treasured. Since we started rewarding our Leaders for good people management based on the results of our people survey and upward feedback we have seen real improvements to our people management practices.

Jenna Stephens, PricewaterhouseCoopers, Global Human Resources Team.

An organisation may be resized, delayered and re-engineered but its competitive edge always relies upon the competency and creativity of its people: that and their motivation to apply themselves in support of their organisation's goals.

It is because of this critical competitive edge that leading organisations are looking to confirm and measure key influences on motivation which affect people's performance in the twenty-first century. By establishing reliable measures they put themselves in the position of being able to monitor the effects of improvement action within their organisation.

Experience shows us that motivating people on a continuous basis is not easy in this rapidly changing world. Some of the factors which managers in one multinational oil company see as influencing the way they need to motivate people are:

Motivating people on a continuous basis is not easy in this rapidly changing world.

- there are more complex problems requiring better cooperation between teams;
- there is more emphasis on respecting individual differences;
- there is more pressure to achieve difficult objectives on time;
- employees and potential employees are becoming better educated;
- higher standards of living are resulting in higher expectations;
- there is a developing demand for more flexible working patterns;
- better medical facilities are enabling people to work productively to a greater age;
- communication technology is becoming more available resulting in increased understanding of what is happening worldwide;
- new levels of political democracy and transparency are developing worldwide;
- businesses are more likely to be subject to reorganisation.

Because of these changing circumstances it is becoming all the more important to ensure senior management regularly monitor the motivation within their organisation and take the necessary action to nurture it.

Here we look at how four leading organisations view the issues of employee motivation, and why they are working to monitor and improve the levels of motivation within their workforce.

TO BE EMPLOYER OF CHOICE

In order to become the dominant consulting firm in the world, one of PricewaterhouseCoopers's strategic objectives is to become the 'employer of choice'. The firm aims to attract the best candidates from all walks of life and retain them long enough to develop their potential to the maximum.

This is not an altruistic approach. PricewaterhouseCoopers's global clients expect the best and if the best is not available, they will look elsewhere. Consequently the ability to attract and retain top-quality consultants is critical to the maintenance of a top-quality client base.

Furthermore high staff turnover impacts significantly on the bottom line. PricewaterhouseCoopers estimate that the cost of employing a new member of staff is between 160–180% of salary. Consequently, in a global professional services firm a relatively small improvement in staff retention reduces the cost of staffing by millions of dollars.

High staff turnover impacts significantly on the bottom line.

> *Every one per cent decrease in staff turnover impacts our bottom line by an estimated $25million.*
>
> Charlie Keeling, Global HR Leader, PricewaterhouseCoopers MCS.

For this reason Senior Partners have invested significant amounts of time in defining the way the firm should do business. Their deliberations have been aimed at surfacing deeply felt business principles which appeal to experienced consultants and top graduates alike.

As part of their people strategy they have designed a measuring instrument called their People Survey, aimed at providing all staff with a 'voice at the table'. The instrument both emphasises MCS's business principles and also enables all staff regularly to highlight where things are going right and where things need to be improved. The results are taken very seriously and lead to focused improvement action.

> *A real issue is understanding the way your people think. As an organisation gets larger it is more difficult to do that. You only know what the ten people nearest to you think – it becomes terribly important to give your people a voice at the table.*
>
> Clive Newton, Senior Partner, PricewaterhouseCoopers.

TO BE A GREAT PLACE TO WORK

BT's Multi-National Sales & Service's goal was to be the most successful service company serving the communication needs of Multi-National customers. To achieve this goal, they relied on the outstanding commitment and motivation of all MNS&S employees and on being able to attract and retain talented people with scarce skills. For this reason they ran a programme of initiatives called 'A Great Place To Work'. They describe what they meant by a great place to work below:

> *We want MNS&S to be an enjoyable and stimulating place to work:*
> - *where professional expertise is valued*
> - *where learning is encouraged*
> - *where everyone is able to give of their best*
> - *where we share and build on each other's ideas*
> - *where people look forward to coming to work.*
>
> MNS&S Management Team

To the senior management team 'a great place to work' meant developing an environment where self-motivation could take root and flourish. In order to build on previous initiatives they decided to create an instrument which would measure how people felt and where resources needed to be focused in the future.

The team supplemented the regular BT surveys with an instrument that specifically measured the characteristics of the Great Place to Work programme. The resulting questionnaire helped identify what activities needed to be put in place to make the Great Place to Work initiative successful and how those activities should be implemented.

TO ENABLE YOUR PEOPLE TO MAKE A DIFFERENCE

Airtours Holidays wants to be the UK's preferred holiday company by leading the way in better quality, value and service. Their people are vital to this success, none more so than those with customer-facing roles throughout the world. The demands of today's holidaymakers require highly motivated people who take the initiative and work effectively as a team.

> *Our regular survey provides real evidence of how our people think and feel. This is vital in helping us to measure our progress as a company. Thoughts, feelings and perceptions of staff are important as well as things like company profits and customer feedback.*
>
> *Developing our people is a key element of our strategy. This means investing in our staff. This we can do more effectively when we have an understanding of the areas we need to work on.*
>
> Chris Mottershead, MD Airtours Holidays, 1997.

They created a measuring instrument aimed at soliciting the views of their staff on those actions that impacted positively on their customers, what could be improved and how people felt about working for the company. It is one of their activities aimed at enabling their people to make a difference.

TO LISTEN, LEARN AND WIN TOGETHER

Elida Fabergé, a wholly owned subsidiary of Unilever, is the largest producer of branded health and beauty products in the UK. The company has always aimed to satisfy the needs of customers (retail outlets) and consumers (users of their products) better than their competitors.

They chose the business excellence model promoted by the European Foundation for Quality Management (EFQM) and the British Quality Foundation (BQF). This model emphasises the need to assess annually a number of key business activities, including how well the organisation manages, develops and releases the knowledge of its people.

> *We want to be a magnet for talent. To achieve this we have to listen to our people and act on what they say.*
>
> Gary Crouch, HR Director, Elida Fabergé.

The Elida Fabergé 'Listening, Learning and Winning Together' survey regularly assesses their people's views on how the organisation is doing in relation to a wide range of areas linked to the business excellence model. From the survey results, continuous improvement plans are established in line with their target of becoming a world-class organisation as measured against the business excellence model.

TO IMPROVE YOUR BUSINESS THROUGH YOUR PEOPLE

> *At one transport company one of our consulting teams carefully quantified the economic penalties of excessive employee churn and found that the client could increase profits 50% by cutting driver turnover in half.*
>
> F.F. Reichheld, Director, Bain & Co.[1]

The actions that are taken by such leading companies provide us with valuable guidelines on what needs to be done to augment the traditional measures of motivation, such as days lost through strikes, sickness and accidents. As we will see, these still have their place, but the emphasis now is towards:

- finding out what issues are current in the minds of employees;
- creating instruments which provide a measure of opinion;
- using their instruments to track motivation;
- taking action as a result of their findings;
- linking the actions with the annual planning cycle.

But does this emphasis on involving people in identifying organisation problems and initiating improvement activities really work? Intuitively it seems right, and it would be unusual for commercially orientated business organisations to invest so much time and effort into measuring motivation if they do not believe a tangible business benefit will emerge. But is there any real proof that it works?

Although it is very difficult to establish research that effectively isolates the 'people factor' from all the others that impact on business performance, there are three outlined below which provide very strong pointers:

- The Sheffield Effectiveness Programme;
- The Institute for Employment Studies Research;
- The Imada Loss Prevention Programme.

The Sheffield Effectiveness Programme found people management practices had the greatest effect on productivity and profitability. Work carried out jointly by the Institute of Work Psychology (University of Sheffield) and the Centre for Economic Performance (London School of Economics) over the last ten years points strongly to a causal linkage between employee motivation and business profitably/productivity.

---

1. Quoted in Reichheld, F. (1996) *The Loyalty Effect*. USA: Boston, MA: Harvard Business School of Publishing.

The study made every effort to compare similar organisations and was rigorously designed to isolate the impact of people on business performance. It came to the conclusion that, when comparing five commonly used managerial practices, one stood out as accounting for the largest variation in business performance.

The researchers calculated the change in company productivity and profitability accounted for by the use of business strategy, emphasis on quality, use of advanced manufacturing technology, use of research and development, and people management. The results indicated very different percentage variations associated with each activity (see Table 1.1).

Table 1.1 Impact of managerial practices on profitability and productivity

	Profitability %	Productivity %
People management practices	17	17
Research and development	8	6
Business strategy	2	3
Emphasis on quality	1	1
Use of advanced technology	1	1

It can be seen from the table that people management practices have by far the most impact on productivity and profitability. The researchers concluded that senior managers should monitor the satisfaction and commitment of employees on a regular basis using standardised surveys, and organisational changes should be made as necessary to promote job satisfaction and employee commitment.

The Institute for Employment Studies Research found better people management increased productivity and sales. The Institute for Employment Studies has carried out two pieces of research which support the proposition that a motivated workforce has an impact on business results. The first research, commissioned by Focus Central London, looked at the impact of implementing Investors in People within central London. The second looked at the impact of employee commitment on retail sales.

Investors in People is a government-backed Business Standard which helps organisations harness their human capital towards meeting business goals. In the past it has been focused primarily on training, but the new standard (introduced in April 2000) is more broadly based and early indications suggest it will be even more successful than earlier versions.

As shown in Figure 1.1 the research carried out indicates a link between the implementation of the Standard, better people management practices and increased productivity and customer satisfaction.

People management practices have by far the most impact on productivity and profitability.

Fig. 1.1 Effect of implementing Investors in People

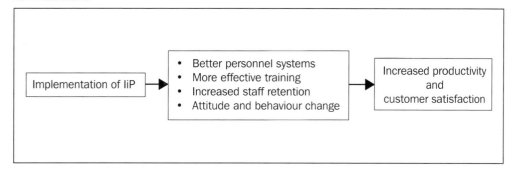

Not unnaturally the researchers also found that the more an organisation had to do to achieve the Standard, the greater the reported positive effect on business performance.

'From People to Profits' describes the Institute of Employment Studies' research into the relationship between employee commitment and retail sales in a major retailer. The researchers correlated measures of employee loyalty, pride and sense of ownership with sales performance data collected over a period of two years. The results indicated a link between employee commitment and changes in sales. IES portrays the link as shown in Figure 1.2.

Fig. 1.2 Link between employee commitment and changes in sales

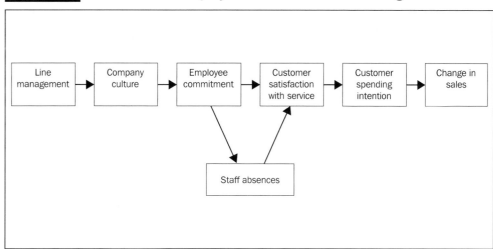

Their calculations indicated that, for the company in question, a one-point increase in employee commitment could lead to a monthly increase of up to £200,000 in sales per store.

> A similar exercise was carried out by Sears Roebuck & Co. in the mid-1990s. They created a rigorous statistical model which was able to predict the impact of employee attitudes on revenue growth.
>
> *If we knew nothing about a local store except that employee attitudes had improved by 5 points on our survey scale, we could predict with confidence that revenue growth would grow by 0.5%. These numbers are as rigorous as any others we work with at Sears. Every year our accounting firm audits them as closely as it audits our financials.*
>
> Rucci, Kirn and Quinn (1998).[2]

The Imada Loss Prevention Programme: cutting costs by 30%

The Imada programme provides another example of how involving people in solving a business problem can impact on the bottom line. In this case work carried out in the transportation division of a multinational petroleum manufacturing organisation focused on the cost of lost days due to injury.

Over a twelve-month period the (already poor) industrial injury frequency had doubled and lost work days quadrupled. The organisation's management decided to examine the issues in the context of the way the organisation operated as a whole.

By carrying out an organisation assessment and subsequently helping to harness the interests and abilities of the employees, management succeeded in:

- reducing lost work days from 1,368 to 42 within five years;

- reducing delivery costs from 2.3 cents to 1.62 cents per gallon over ten years.

This latter figure represents a 30 per cent cost saving per gallon over 2.2 billion gallons per year compounded.

Some of the management practices Imada recommended for improvement are listed below:

- increased control by employees over their work;

- employee participation in the recruitment and selection process;

- employee involvement in workplace and equipment design;

---

2. Rucci, A.J., Kirn, S.P. and Quinn, R.T. (1998) 'The Employee – Customer – Profit Chain at Sears', in D. Ulrich (ed.), *Delivering Results*. USA: Boston, MA: Harvard Business School Publishing.

- changes to the purchasing of equipment;
- use of experienced employees as trainers;
- better information sharing and feedback;
- better communication between teams;
- additional non-technical skills training;
- use of focused performance measures.

It can be seen that the majority are related to good management of people. A summary of the resulting changes is given in Table 1.2.

Table 1.2   Imada: summary of resulting changes

What it was like before	What it is like now
Matrix organisation	Local teamwork led by local managers
Paternal organisation	Success dependent on local leadership
Employees told what to do	Employees plan, decide and act
Productivity low	Culture of continuous improvement
Plant and equipment unreliable	Plant and equipment second to none
Loyal employees	Loyal employees

These three pieces of work do not necessarily provide conclusive evidence of the linkage between employee motivation and business results. There are also a number of research projects which have failed to identify a correlation. There is enough to support the view that investing in good human resource management practices can generate significant benefits – but organisations cannot afford to make a half-hearted attempt on this front.

Investing in good human resource management practices can generate significant benefits.

KEY POINT SUMMARY

- An organisation's competitive edge always relies on the competency and creativity of its people and their motivation to apply themselves in support of their organisation's goals.
- Experience shows us that motivating people on a continuous basis is not easy.
- Consequently it is becoming all the more important to ensure you regularly monitor motivation within your organisation and take the necessary action to nurture it.

- The four main contributor organisations are doing just this in order to:
  - be employer of choice;
  - be a great place to work;
  - enable people to make a difference;
  - to listen, learn, and win.
- Although research results are variable, there is hard evidence accumulating to confirm that a motivated workforce has a measurable impact on business results.

2

Common influences on motivation

The last chapter explained that forward-looking organisations assess what factors influence the motivation of their employees, monitor them and take appropriate improvement action. This chapter looks at what issues are commonly found to motivate, or demotivate.

Typically at any given time organisations asking their people about motivation find a range of 'hot issues'. These 'hot issues' differ depending at what stage of development the organisation is in and the seniority of people asked.

In creating a measuring instrument it is important to reflect these current 'hot issues'. But it is also important to include issues that may not be currently uppermost in the minds of employees – by doing so it is possible to establish an instrument which is balanced and which can be used regularly over the years.

> The questionnaire focuses on the issues we think are most important to you, the things closest to our hearts. These include:
>
> - work and time – creating a balanced lifestyle
> - feeling valued as a person and for your contributions
> - recognition and reward
> - leadership
> - administrative support and communications
> - working environment
> - opportunities for professional and personal growth.
>
> PricewaterhouseCoopers questionnaire.

There are recurring themes which can be found in many organisations and consequently need to be part of a measuring instrument. At the time of instrument design some may be 'hot', others less so.

In the review of these recurring themes below some associated quotations from employees who have commented on their organisations have been selected. The quotations do not all come from the four main contributors to this book.

There must be few senior managers now who have not come across the work of Herzberg. His research into motivation was one of the first to create a distinction between a 'motivator' and a 'hygiene factor', the latter now commonly called a 'satisfier'.

Motivators broadly are those factors which actively harness interests and abilities. Satisfiers simply demotivate if they are not there – but do not motivate if they are.

All the issues below, both motivators and satisfiers, affect individual motivation – but not all employees will be affected at the same time, or by the same issue.

Furthermore there is not full agreement on which are satisfiers and which are motivators. Indeed, it is possible that a satisfier in one company could be a motivator in another.

For example, job security is usually thought to be a satisfier, but in some companies employees know that 'not delivering the goods' has an immediate and strong influence on company survival. Hence in their case job security is a motivator.

The common influences are depicted in Figure 2.1.

Fig. 2.1   Common influences on motivation

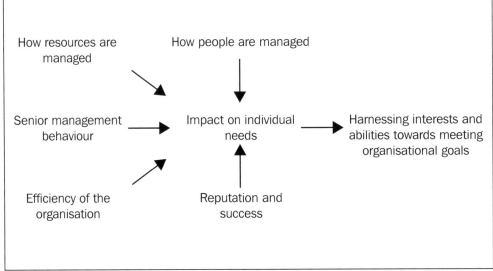

SENIOR MANAGEMENT BEHAVIOUR

Dig deep enough into the reasons for a poorly motivated workforce and it is usually the senior management that are to blame.

It is usually the senior management that are to blame.

The comment below shows how a senior management team, working hard to keep their business competitive and consequently making unpopular decisions, were viewed by one respondent:

> *Please remember that directors lead – which means they show the way. (I know you know this but your behaviour prompts this reminder.) Last year I was unimpressed by your behaviour – and the values implicit in your behaviour. Now, sadly, I know the colour of your cloth. Subject to any change you wish to make that is.*
>
> Anonymous.

The way people see their senior management is critical to motivation. Some of the key leadership issues are:

- direction
- visibility
- proactivity
- perception of fairness
- perception of teamwork
- consistency.

Together they create an environment where, with good day-to-day supervision, self-motivation can flourish.

Providing direction

I do not believe my line management have set clear goals for their part of the business. Everything stems from that.

Anonymous.

It is really self-evident – or should be – that the senior managers should regularly communicate the direction in which the organisation is heading. Lack of direction can be a major 'turn off' for potential movers and shakers and can also result in a significant amount of effort being directed at the wrong goal.

Since I joined the business I have been part of a focused, forward-looking, progressive and highly motivated team. The senior managers communicate regularly with the team, providing direction, support and encouragement when needed.

Anonymous.

Being visible

It is common for senior managers to focus on urgent issues of, for example sales, finance, litigation and public relations. Their people are seen as important, of course ('people are our most important asset'), but unless there is a compelling reason to focus on people (strikes, go-slows, team defections), often the senior manager tackles the urgent issues and leaves the important ones to look after themselves.

> *Hello, is there anyone up there? Do we have any directors? I haven't seen any in the last year.*
>
> Anonymous.

Being proactive

People expect their senior managers to spot future trends that are likely to impact on the organisation, and not to be 'wrong footed' too often. They like to be associated with forward-looking organisations because this can have a big impact on their self-image and help improve the chances of a relatively secure job.

Establishing a perception of fairness

Senior management are expected to create a culture of perceived fairness. This includes:

- ensuring equal opportunities for appointments;
- ensuring fairness of pay and conditions;
- ensuring fairness in dealing with 'people issues';
- being honest and consistent in what they say and do;
- fostering an environment of trust and cooperation.

> *I know that people doing a similar job to me are being paid much more in another department. I have spoken to my manager about this but she doesn't want to know. I really feel this is unfair.*
>
> Anonymous.

This perception of fairness – or lack of perceived fairness – is one of the most regularly cited 'hot issues'.

Working as a top team

If the senior management team appears to lack teamwork, then this can often cascade through the organisation and create inappropriate conflict. Inappropriate conflict results in poor cooperation between different parts of the organisation, and this saps the will to perform.

There is a sense of lack of leadership and in-fighting at the top. The effect filters down.

Anonymous.

There is no joined up thinking at senior management level.

Anonymous.

Creating consistency in treatment of people

People also like to know where their organisation stands on important matters, such as quality, environment, health and safety, recruitment, training and development, work–life balance, etc., and clear policy statements are a good first step. Where organisations have no 'thought through' policies on such issues then it is less likely that managers and front-line staff will be able to make correct and consistent decisions within their sphere of operations. Lack of consistency is a major demotivator. The box below shows one organisation's policy statement.

Sharing in the future of our business

We will create and maintain an environment in which individual employees may contribute to and share in the fortunes of the business in a fair and consistent manner.

As an employee you can expect to:

- be informed of what your role and tasks are;
- be appropriately trained and developed for the role and tasks required of you;
- be allowed the opportunity to perform;
- be regularly counselled on how you are doing and what your potential is;
- be recognised and rewarded according to your individual achievements;
- be managed professionally;
- be given the willing assistance and support of your colleagues to the extent of your ability;
- be informed of what your company is doing and what its objectives are;

Continued

- know that we actively encourage promotion from within the company;
- have your ideas and opinions properly considered;
- not be burdened by those not willing to contribute.

Anonymous policy statement.

HOW PEOPLE ARE MANAGED

Senior management provide a framework – create an environment – for how people are managed, but it is the rest of the managers and supervisors who manage individuals and teams on a day-to-day basis. Some of the competencies of a good people manager are shown in the boxes below which summarise the feedback from focus groups.

BT MNS&S – what employees expect of a manager

- Communicates openly and honestly.
- Is consistent and trustworthy.
- Practises what is preached.
- Listens to and values individuals.
- Involves the team in the decision-making process.
- Coaches and gives constructive feedback.
- Admits mistakes and learns from them.
- Honours promises and commitments.
- Regards other teams as colleagues not competitors.

What PricewaterhouseCoopers expects of its leaders

- Provide a clear sense of direction.
- Emphasise the importance of doing the best work possible.
- Encourage people to contribute ideas and suggestions.
- Encourage people to learn from you.
- Provide constructive feedback.

Continued

- Initiate action.

- Respond to problems quickly.

- Show team members they are valuable.

- Show strong positive relationships are important.

- Conduct meetings to emphasise trust and respect.

- Help team members balance their business and personal life.

- Encourage respect for people regardless of their background.

- Be available to give support when needed.

- Share knowledge with other teams.

- Take responsibility for your decisions.

- Display high standards of ethical behaviour and professionalism.

'Good management' of people is inherently difficult because different people are motivated by different things at different times in their lives. But there are still useful rules of thumb that can be flexed to cater for the individual. These include:

- appointing the right people for the job;

- making sure people are properly introduced to the organisation;

- providing a healthy and safe environment – physical and emotional;

- ensuring job design links with organisational objectives;

- discussing what constitutes 'good performance' and providing feedback;

- giving regular advice and encouragement;

- helping keep knowledge and skills up to date;

- involving them in dialogue and decision making;

- enabling them to 'grow' within the organisation;

- recognising effort and success.

'Good management' of people is inherently difficult because different people are motivated by different things at different times in their lives.

The manager I work under is the best manager that I have worked with in my working life. He brought me into the organisation and has always been there when needed. I enjoy working here and hope that in the years to come I can be where my manager is now.

Anonymous.

Appointing the right people for the job

Perhaps the most demotivating thing that can happen to an individual is to be appointed to carry out a job for which he or she is not suited. Many people can tackle such jobs for short periods of time, and it is sometimes of benefit to the individual, for example in the case of management development. But there are many people who are poorly appointed, and in the era of sophisticated assessment techniques, it is the organisation that should take the lion's share of the blame.

> The manager had been working in sales for over two years now – a promotion from a successful market research job. He was being assessed for fast-track development when the assessor spotted an unusual score on the stress scale of a personality instrument. When asked about the unusual score the manager broke down. He had been promoted to a high customer contact job, but was a strong introvert. He (a French speaker) had been moved to French-speaking Canada – but his wife did not speak French and had difficulty learning it. The manager was living in pure hell at home and work and could see no way out.

Making sure people are properly introduced into the organisation

Most successful new recruits approach their work highly motivated to succeed, if a little apprehensive. If they are not motivated, then the appointments system probably is at fault. The best way to ensure that motivation is soon dissipated is to leave people to sink or swim. An effective introduction to the organisation, its mission, products and services, values, systems and procedures ensures a new recruit becomes productive earlier – and is impressed.

> *As a new person in the team, I am thoroughly enjoying my role and am satisfied with the level of support and encouragement I receive.*
>
> Anonymous.

Providing a healthy and safe environment – physical and emotional

On the physical side, when it comes to motivation, health and safety issues constitute a double-edged sword. For example, traditional health and safety issues such as machine guards can reduce output and therefore be disliked by operatives. This is particularly so when output is linked to pay.

The more modern issues associated with continuous use of computers can have a major adverse effect on performance. The development of eyestrain, recurring headaches, worsening backache and strained tendons can be both demotivating and debilitating.

Associated with the emotional side is the current 'hot issue' of work–life balance. Most motivated employees will work long hours when asked, but continued unsociable hours at the expense of family life are not attractive to those with families.

> *There is a lot of lip service paid to the balance between work and personal life, but when it comes to the crunch there is an expectation that everything else in life takes second place to work.*
>
> Anonymous.

Also on the emotional side, for many people there is a strong need to 'belong' both to their team and their organisation as a whole. People with strong emotional ties to their team (friendships and happy memories) tend to enjoy their work and stay loyal.

> *I feel absolutely no loyalty or belonging to my team as there are currently no mechanisms, socially or professionally, operating to create a good team spirit.*
>
> Anonymous.

Ensuring job design links with organisation objectives

People are motivated when they know how their job contributes to the overall business goals. Consequently it is important to ensure that the objectives and key result areas of a job are aligned to business goals.

> The labourer had been working for a vehicle manufacturer – doing the same job for nearly 35 years. When asked what he had been doing for 35 years the man answered 'screwing nuts onto bolts'. When asked why, he answered 'damned if I know but it pays the bills'.

Discussing and agreeing what constitutes 'good performance'

Understanding and agreeing with personal goals, and understanding what needs to be done to achieve them is a major predeterminant of motivation. Get this right, together with good job design (above) and a job holder can survive many demotivators.

> *Management need to articulate short-term goals. There is an obvious gap between our high-level aims and what we personally are expected to contribute.*
>
> Anonymous.

Giving them regular advice and encouragement

Unless the job holder is an old hand it is likely that he or she will value coaching from his or her manager – the best way of learning is often found to be 'on the job'. Coaching should help people reach peak performance through knowing where they fit into the overall picture and how they can best contribute to the performance of their team.

'I only get told when things go wrong' is a popular comment from focus groups.

Helping keep their knowledge and skills up to date

One of the most important motivators is the provision of opportunities to keep abreast of developments affecting people's work. This is because knowledge soon becomes out of date with advances in science and technology. This, together with the demise of 'jobs for life', means people put high value on opportunities for education and development.

Involving them in dialogue and decision-making

Mushroom management – keeping people in the dark etc. – is a recipe for disaster in today's work environment. Most (though not all) people insist on being informed and involved in decision-making affecting their work.

> *I often feel that my opinions on certain matters do not count as much as other members of the team, in that decisions are made without consulting or gathering ideas and opinions from all team members.*
>
> Anonymous.

Enabling them to 'grow' within the organisation

As an organisation develops and grows, people (though not all) want to develop and grow with it. In addition to keeping their knowledge and skills up to date, they want to learn new things that enable them to climb the promotion ladder. For these people, lack of opportunity is a reason for finding pastures new.

> *I am new to the organisation and very happy and motivated to be working here. I believe that it would be a good idea to map out the potential development levels of individuals long term and not simply for a twelve-month period. I understand this would be vague and flexible, but it may give people the opportunity to see how their careers may progress.*
>
> Anonymous.

Recognising effort and success

Good pay and benefits are not necessarily motivating to people but can be demotivating if people think they are unfairly remunerated.

Pay can be a motivator if part of it is variable and linked to performance – and the criteria for good performance are seen to be fair.

One strong motivator which costs very little is non-financial recognition. People generally respond positively to both formal recognition systems and informal thanks from leaders they respect.

> *At the end of the day we all want to be treated as 'humans' and managers do need to appreciate when people are giving the best of their ability.*
>
> Anonymous.

THE EFFICIENCY OF THE ORGANISATION

An inefficient organisation is no breeding ground for motivated people. Characteristics of inefficient organisations include:

- long and involved processes;
- decisions being taken at too high a level;
- turf wars dissipating energy.

An inefficient organisation is no breeding ground for motivated people.

Involved or bureaucratic processes block organisational arteries

In the past, few critical business processes were actively designed to be effective and efficient. Traditionally parts of key business processes grew up in different departments and no one took a bird's eye view of the relevance and sequencing of activities. Consequently the range of activities constituting the arteries of the organisation were subject to inefficiencies such as inappropriate red tape, stockpiling and duplication of effort.

With the introduction of business process management these issues are becoming less prevalent – but do still exist.

> *The biggest challenge we face is information management. We do not have a single database to interrogate. The second biggest challenge is getting to grips with 'e-'.*
>
> *Also, if our finance systems developers had been real suppliers they would probably have been sacked for gross and persistent incapability.*
>
> Anonymous.

Decisions taken at too high a level disenfranchise people

With people becoming better educated (probably) and better informed (certainly) there comes an expectation that decisions affecting their work will be made at the level where the problems arise. Where this is not so, and associated management style is autocratic, then the organisation runs the risk of its people feeling disenfranchised.

> *The organisation should concentrate on using the skills and experience of its staff, and empowering those on temporary projects. Frankly a lot of us are sitting around on our bottoms bored out of our trees.*
>
> Anonymous.

Poor management of key resources, has an impact on motivation.

Turf wars dissipate goal-achieving energy

Long and involved processes are often due to a strong departmental structure. This in turn encourages management 'growing up in tubes' (the accounts clerk becomes accounts manager, having spent 20 years in the same department) and the risk of a blinkered view of organisational issues. The attention of managers is focused more on protecting their patch, less on meeting organisational goals. That focus permeates the department as a whole and inappropriate organisational conflict flourishes.

> *The structure of the organisation encourages empire building, doubling up of functions leading to conflict and consequent staff dissatisfaction – and the loss of good people.*
>
> Anonymous.

The above three issues do not necessarily reduce motivation *per se*. Some people will work long hours doing the wrong thing well. Others will take delight in not having to make a decision and spend valuable time working out ways to 'get one over' on the next door department. But this does not harness interests and abilities to meet organisational goals.

HOW RESOURCES ARE MANAGED

Poor management of key resources, including finance, information, suppliers, partners, materials, equipment, energy, buildings, etc., has an impact on motivation. Some of the issues which regularly crop up are:

- investment in the future (or lack of it);
- knowledge of the business (or lack of it);
- equipment/tools to do the job (not up to date);
- buildings and workstations (not suitable for the job).

Investing in the future

Knowledge that investment in the future exists provides the comfort of believing there is going to be a future, and can also help generate pride in belonging. It is not unknown for investment decisions to be restricted to the board – sometimes for good commercial reasons – but if it is possible to divulge some information, people are heartened that the directors are investing for the future.

> *Before I started work with the company I searched aimlessly for a job that would mean something to me. Now I know I can look to the future and grow as the company grows. I plan to make this company my career. Thank you.*
>
> Anonymous.

Managing knowledge in the business

Information and knowledge are major resources as the proliferation of 'knowledge management' initiatives demonstrates. There are some types of knowledge which are inherently motivating because the fact that people are 'in the know' provides them with a sense of self-worth. Lack of knowledge required to do the job in hand (changing priorities, new products, revised schedules) can sap energy and initiative. So too can poorly prioritised information which overwhelms recipients with too many facts.

> *My boss is absolutely great to work with. He treats me with respect and gives me every opportunity to learn as much about the company as I want to learn and be involved in.*
>
> Anonymous.

Providing equipment/tools to do the job

These are not motivators in themselves, but can be demotivators if they are not up to date. In organisations aspiring to be best in class, the availability of up-to-date equipment and associated support is a necessity for motivated performance.

The self-image of people links with their job and the organisation in which they work.

> *Every single time I have tried to get help from Technical Support they have been polite, cooperative and completely useless.*
>
> Anonymous.

As we shall see in Chapter 9, over the years, and prompted by the results of their surveys, PricewaterhouseCoopers MCS has ensured that all their people have both access to suitable IT facilities (laptops for frequent travellers) together with good technical support.

Providing suitable buildings and workstations

Once again these are not motivators but can generate demotivation if they are not suitable for the work in hand.

> *An additional issue requiring urgent attention is the state of our work space. It is the most depressing area I have ever worked in...*
>
> Anonymous.

REPUTATION AND SUCCESS

The self-image of people links with their job and the organisation in which they work. Consequently the organisation's reputation can have a major impact on motivation.

> *I feel I work for the best company on the planet. The company tries its best to keep us happy and also cares very much for the customer, and does an excellent job. I am proud to work for this organisation and hope we are successful with our vision for the future.*
>
> Anonymous.

Reputation takes a long time to build but very little time to destroy and it is important to monitor how the organisation is seen internally in terms of being:

- a good employer;
- forward looking;
- caring neighbour;
- successful in what it does.

A good employer is seen as offering predictable employment and an opportunity to develop and maintaining marketable competencies, good working conditions and competitive conditions of employment.

Forward looking means demonstrating through, for example, an innovative product range, investment in technology and participative management style that the organisation means to survive and prosper in the years to come.

A caring neighbour manages potential environmental impact sensitively and supports local neighbourhood initiatives.

A company seen to be successful in what it does manages public relations, investor relations and customer relations successfully, and is seen to be successful by the media.

The trick for a senior management team is to provide a physical and psychological environment where these diverse interests and abilities can be continuously harnessed.

INFLUENCING WHAT EXACTLY?

So far we have been looking at the influences that organisations which measure motivation have identified as relevant. We have also defined the concept of motivation as 'interests and abilities harnessed towards meeting organisational goals'. But what exactly are these interests and abilities? What is it that influences are influencing?

Many surveys ask respondents to rank the aspects of motivation which they judge as important. The results indicate that a wide range of interests and abilities are potentially influenced.

Looking at individual responses it is clear that different people are motivated by different influences at different times in their career. The trick for a senior management team is to provide a physical and psychological environment where these diverse interests and abilities can be continuously harnessed. The interests include the following.

Structure and predictability

Most people need to have some structure and predictability in their life, and work is usually the primary source: where to go, what to do, how well to do it, what is important/unimportant, what is going to happen tomorrow, how to pay the bills each month, etc.

Contact with people

For many people work offers their main source of companionship and relationships. Indeed some individuals see their friends at work as their anchor in the storms of life. Additionally some people get a buzz out of forming transitory or business relationships – salespeople and negotiators are a case in point.

Rewards and recognition

This is one of the critical needs in the sense that the vast majority of people are motivated by rewards for effort and results. Most measuring instruments find that respondents do not feel adequately rewarded or recognised for extra effort or results. One culprit is reward systems which do not cater for variable pay over and above the basic. But money is not the only reward people value – non-financial rewards can also be powerful motivators.

Influence

People like to influence what happens in their workplace. The need ranges from the clerical worker who wants to have a say where the new photocopier should be placed to the manager who wants to contribute to the annual business plan. The concept of empowerment recognises this need, but there are still many people at work who feel powerless – and consequently not motivated to act.

Achievement

People at work like to see the results of their efforts. Once again this can range from the managing director who can report improved business results to the holiday representative who receives glowing feedback from satisfied holidaymakers. This need is reflected in one of the important components of total quality management – everyone should have the equivalent of a 'speedometer': a measuring instrument to give them feedback on how they are doing.

Pride in belonging

People like to 'belong', and preferably to a group in which they can take pride. This can range from pride in belonging to an organisation that has won the British Quality Award to pride in belonging to a successful team in any given organisation.

Personal growth

As well as being a requirement for survival in a fast-moving world, personal growth is often seen as a personal need – many people have a thirst for know-how which transcends most other motivators. For them it is a need which has to be continually satisfied.

Figure 2.2 gives an indication as to which of the influences listed in this chapter can have an impact on individual needs.

Fig. 2.2 Impact of influences on employee needs

Influences \ Impact on employee need for …	Structure and predictability	Contact with people	Reward and recognition	Influence	Achievement	Pride	Personal growth
Senior management behaviour	✓		✓			✓	
How people are managed	✓	✓	✓	✓	✓	✓	✓
How efficient the organisation is	✓				✓	✓	
How resources are managed	✓		✓	✓	✓	✓	
Reputation and success	✓		✓	✓	✓	✓	✓

DIFFERENT STROKES FOR DIFFERENT FOLKS

The strength of the influences on motivation differs according to the type of organisation, the department within an organisation and the state the organisation is in. There is really no substitute for finding out for yourself what the key motivators and demotivators are within the different parts of your organisation.

Find out for yourself what the key motivators and demotivators are within the different parts of your organisation.

Different organisations

For example, Table 2.1 shows the major influences on motivation as defined by a group of professional staff and a group of factory staff.

Table 2.1 Top motivators and dissatisfiers among professional and factory staff

Professional staff	Factory staff
Top motivators	*Top motivators*
1. Challenging work	1. Being treated with respect
2. People I work with	2. Having management I can respect
3. Career development opportunities	3. Job security
Top dissatisfiers	*Top dissatisfiers*
1. Pressure of work	1. Opportunities for advancement
	2. Lack of recognition

Different departments

Within an organisation there are also differences in what people see as being motivators and demotivators.

The results from a car dealership are a case in point. The figures in Table 2.2 show the rank order of how their people saw the importance of seven influences. They are divided into four different departments – sales, service, parts and technical.

All staff are in agreement that the work they do and the people they work for are the most important, and all rank the friendly atmosphere fourth. But there are some differences which would be of interest to the senior management team – sales staff, for example, have rated job security as least important while parts and technical see it as their number three priority.

Table 2.2 Ranking of influences in different departments

All depts	Major motivators	Sales	Service	Parts	Tech.
1	The work I do	1	2	2	1
2	The people I work with	2	1	1	2
3	The friendly atmosphere	4	4	4	4
4	Our reputation	3	3	5	6
5	Job security	7	5	3	3
6	Salary/benefits package	5	6	6	7
7	Career opportunities	6	7	7	5

When asked about the demotivators there is another set of differences and less unanimity (see Table 2.3). Parts and technical feel 'over-managed' while in sales it is the length of working hours which seems to be causing pain. On the other hand the long hours are relatively well rewarded by the look of it – but not if you work outside of sales.

Table 2.3 Ranking of demotivators

All depts	Major demotivators	Sales	Service	Parts	Tech.
1	Over-management	5	4	1	2
2	Poor salary/benefits	6	1	2	1
3	Pressure of work	2	3	3	4
4	Feeling exploited	3	2	6	3
5	Length of working hours	1	4	4	7
6	Under-management	4	7	7	8
7	Feeling of job insecurity	8	6	8	6
8	Lack of praise/recognition	7	8	5	5

KEY POINT SUMMARY

- If employees are asked about motivation there are recurring themes that can be found.
- The recurring themes – issues which impact on employee motivation – are:
  - senior management behaviour;
  - how people are managed;

    – the efficiency of the organisation;

    – how resources are managed;

    – reputation and success.

- In a given organisation at any given time there will be 'hot issues' which are at the forefront of employees' minds.

- It is important to design a balanced measuring instrument which includes both the current 'hot issues' plus others that are known to impact on motivation.

- All motivators and demotivators impact on individuals' personal needs and affect how much interest and energy they invest in helping to meet organisational goals.

3

Putting the measurement in context

The last two chapters indicate that, in order to achieve and maintain a competitive edge, forward-looking organisations are focusing on the motivation of their people. The key influences on motivation have been outlined and it has been explained that all influences need to be included in a balanced measuring instrument.

To achieve maximum effect for the instrument, the results obtained need to be integrated into a selection of measures used to monitor overall organisational performance. This chapter looks at how the four example organisations achieve this integration.

THE AIRTOURS HOLIDAYS APPROACH

One of Airtours Holidays' strategic goals is to enable their people to make a difference. This strategic goal is recognised within the company as the one which will underpin all objectives and is essential to both its business success and achieving its vision.

From this strategic goal – enabling people to make a difference – they have identified four objectives which are incorporated into their balanced scorecard:

- establish and develop an effective culture which supports the business;

- have a clearly communicated business strategy;

- develop a high-performance environment;

- have people who 'live the values'.

Airtours identifies three types of activity they use to monitor the achievement of these objectives:

- *face-to-face meetings,* including directors' briefings, team briefings, employee forums and focus groups;

- *structured feedback,* including an organisation climate inventory, 360° feedback, customer service questionnaires and their Viewpoint employee survey;

- *performance management,* including cascading business goals into personal objectives, the use of 'one to ones' to review progress, and formal reviews every six months.

Their Viewpoint survey has evolved over the last few years and is now designed around the organisation's values and the behaviours that underpin them. Those values are:

- organised and professional;

- creative and inspiring;

> Their Viewpoint survey is now designed around the organisation's values and the behaviours that underpin them.

- friendly and enthusiastic;

- genuine and trustworthy.

The approach is summarised in Figure 3.1.

Fig. 3.1 The Airtours Holidays approach

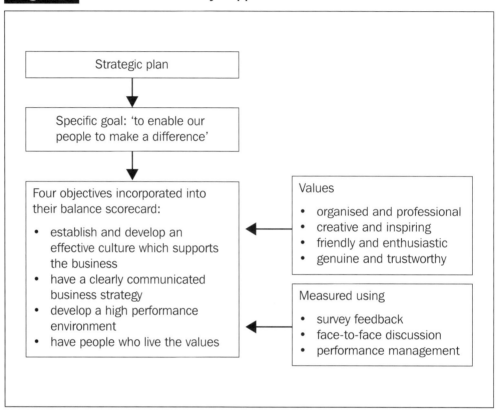

THE BT MULTI-NATIONAL SALES AND SERVICE APPROACH

Like all four contributors, the BT MNS&S senior management team attached enormous importance to the concept of customer loyalty and put in place a number of activities to drive up customer loyalty.

As part of these activities they developed a measurement tool called the Performance and Partnership Index to provide an overall index figure relating to key customers, incorporating data from a number of existing sources. The constituents of the index were called loyalty drivers and included measures of:

- customer satisfaction;

- organisation image;

- customer relationships;

They developed a
measurement tool
called the
Performance and
Partnership Index.

- customer complaints;
- customer expectations;
- competitor perception;
- employee motivation.

The survey instrument they created was used to fine-tune a number of programmes that were already underway, including initiatives designed to increase the motivation and commitment of employees. Figure 3.2 demonstrates how the instrument linked to the Performance and Partnership Index, and outlines the factors that were felt to influence motivation in MNS&S.

Fig 3.2   The BT MNS&S approach

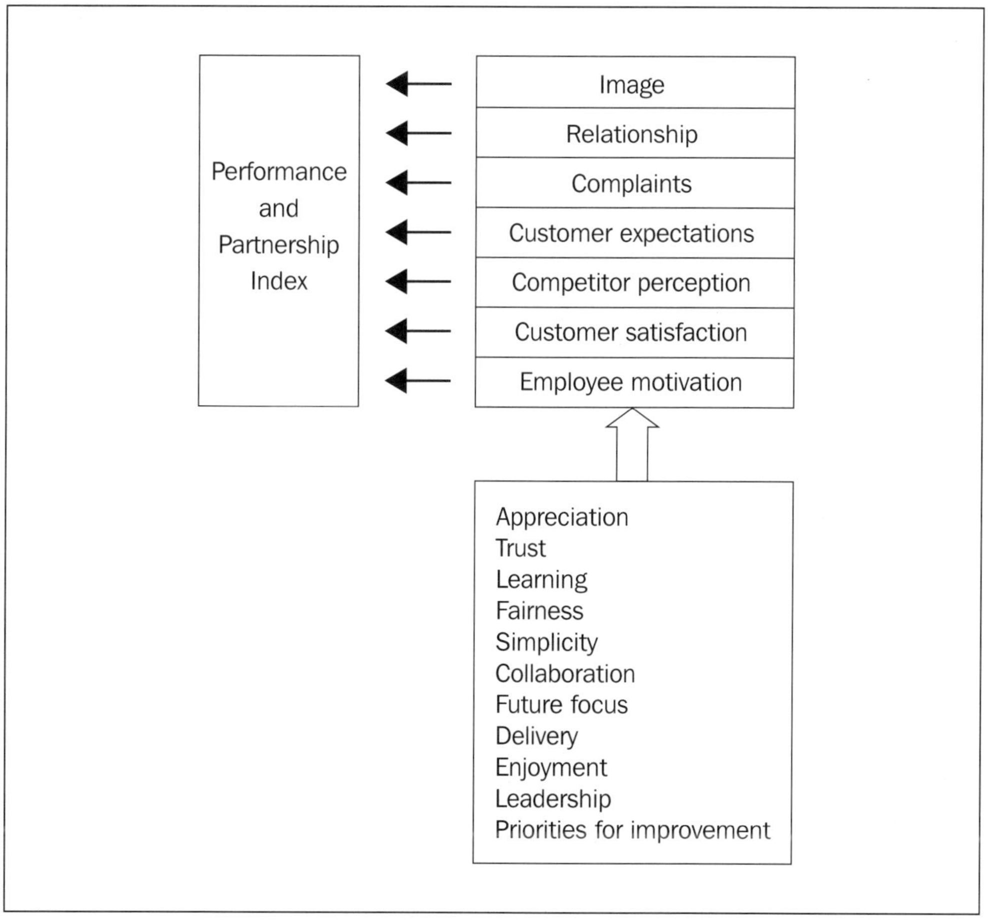

THE ELIDA FABERGÉ APPROACH

The Elida Fabergé senior management team use the Business Excellence Model promoted by the European Foundation for Quality Management and the British Quality Foundation as a framework for regular self-assessment and continuous improvement. The 1998 model shown in Figure 3.3 also indicates the percentage weighting given to each element when an assessment of an organisation is carried out.

Fig. 3.3 The Elida Fabergé approach

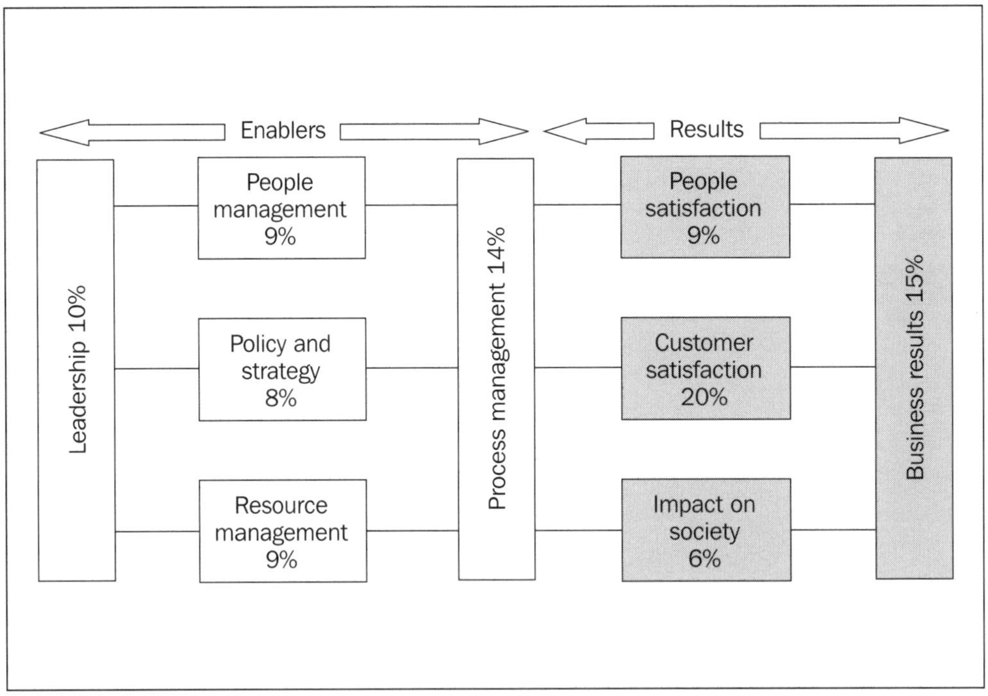

Their goals include:

- becoming a world-class organisation which, in the context of the Business Excellence Model, means boosting their performance on each of the elements above; and

- achieving sustained profitable growth.

Over the last four years they have made significant progress towards both.

The Elida Fabergé 'Listening, Learning, Winning Together Survey' was designed to help measure how the company was doing in relation to the different elements of the model, and particularly in relation to people satisfaction.

Their survey is used every two years with questions grouped according to the elements of the Excellence Model. This reinforces the linkages between people satisfaction and business excellence ensuring that the survey is seen as a mainstream activity.

The Elida Fabergé senior management team use the Business Excellence Model as a framework.

THE PRICEWATERHOUSECOOPERS MCS APPROACH

One of PricewaterhouseCoopers' strategic objectives is to be 'employer of choice'. In order to achieve this they have emphasised the need to focus on developing people. This is reflected in their Balanced Scorecard for Leaders of Business Units (see Figure 3.4).

Fig. 3.4   **The PricewaterhouseCoopers approach**

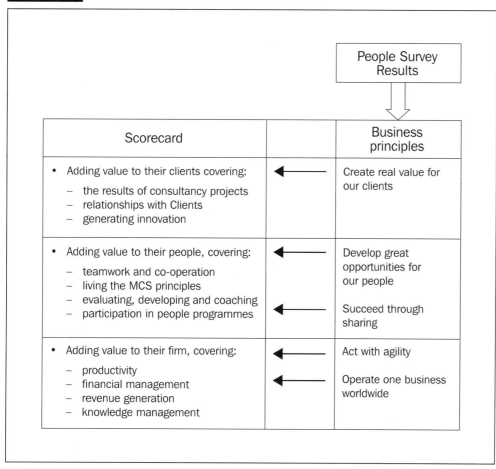

Their People Survey is designed around their five main business principles.

Their People Survey contributes to the balanced score card and is designed around their five main business principles:

- create real value for our clients;

- operate as one business world-wide;

- develop great opportunities for our people;

- succeed through sharing; and

- act with agility.

The people survey aims to assess how advanced the business units within MCS are in working towards their business principles, and these link directly with the critical success factors contained within their balanced scorecards.

PricewaterhouseCoopers use their survey annually to help monitor how well they are operating based on their business principles.

KEY POINT SUMMARY

- To achieve maximum effect for your measuring instrument, the results obtained need to be part of a selection of measures used to monitor organisation performance.

- Airtours Holidays does this by monitoring the achievement of specific people management objectives which are part of their Balanced Scorecard

- BT Multi-National Sales and Service created a Performance and Partnership Index which included measures of image, customer relationships, customer complaints, customer expectations, competitor perception, customer satisfaction and employee motivation.

- Elida Fabergé link their results with the business excellence model covering leadership, people management, policy and strategy, resource management, process management, customer satisfaction, impact on society and business results as well as people satisfaction.

- PwC link their survey results to their Balanced Scorecard. Both the structure of their survey and their scorecard are based on business principles which are used throughout their organisation.

Unless you are tasked with designing and delivering your measure of motivation, you can now move on to Chapter 8. Those who are responsible for delivering a set of measures need to continue with Chapters 4 to 7.

Creating the measurement instrument

So far we have looked at reasons for measuring motivation and those factors which influence motivation, and indicated that any measurements created should be part of a selection which monitor the performance of an organisation. Here we look at the techniques used for measuring motivation. It is not necessary to read this chapter unless you are tasked with delivering a measure of motivation.

Measuring motivation can be done in two ways:

■ *The first and most common approach is to use a selection of 'hard' measures.* This approach is common because, historically, personnel departments have kept records of, for example, employee turnover and days lost through strikes, etc. The historical approach tended to concentrate on levels of dissatisfaction, but it is becoming more common now to choose numbers which monitor motivation, not simply lack of dissatisfaction. These are discussed in more detail below.

■ *The second approach is to use specially designed questionnaires*, or instruments, which cover a wide range of motivators and satisfiers. Organisations on the leading edge of this approach issue their questionnaires on a regular basis to track and anticipate changes in sentiment.

USING BOTH HARD AND SOFT MEASURES

Hard measures focusing on satisfiers are probably the easiest to pinpoint because in all likelihood they already exist in one form or another, and probably already have industry benchmarks. Examples of hard measures focusing on employee satisfaction include:

■ employee turnover;

■ days lost through strikes;

■ days lost through ill health;

■ days lost through accidents;

■ number of grievances.

> The current emphasis is to find hard measures which focus on employee motivation.

As explained above, the current emphasis is to find hard measures which focus on employee motivation, and the choice of these tends to reflect the culture of the organisation. Examples include:

■ percentage of people accepting/rejecting job offers;

■ percentage of vacancies filled through internal promotion;

■ number of training days per year;

■ reduction in overall competency gaps;

- level of use of suggestion schemes;

- numbers of people involved in improvement teams;

- number of formally recognised successes;

- number of director walkabouts.

Examples of hard measures used by Elida Fabergé

- Average time in job

- Average training days per employee

- Percentage absenteeism

- Percentage employee turnover – managerial/non-managerial

- Percentage eligible for good service awards

- Number of lost time accidents

- Percentage use of the employee assistance programme

- Number of personal development plans implemented

The use of soft measures is less common, and it is on this aspect that this book concentrates. Survey technology has been used for a number of different purposes in the past (e.g. defining different organisational cultures, catalysing change, communicating a change in policy), and before any such instrument is created it is important to agree its role within your organisation.

AGREEING THE ROLE OF THE SURVEY INSTRUMENT

In this book it is assumed that the role is to:

- identify key influences on motivation;

- measure the key influences;

- provide a means of prioritising improvement action;

and, by doing this, improve motivation within an organisation.

Many diverse purposes can be encompassed with this remit, but it is a useful exercise to set down in writing the reasons for establishing a capability to measure motivation.

Creating a measure for an organisation's critical success factors is a demanding job. An instrument for measuring such an elusive concept as motivation is no less demanding. Consequently, in order to create a valid and fair instrument it is usually best not to leave the job to one person – good practice is to set up a measurement team.

SETTING UP THE MEASUREMENT TEAM

The measurement team should be the senior management team or a project team reporting directly to the senior management team. The critical issue is to ensure that there is support for the use of a measuring instrument from key organisation decision-makers. Lip service alone is likely to result in a poor employee reaction.

How not to set it up

Give the responsibility to one manager – preferably in 'personnel' so that 'line' can wash its hands of the issue – and preferably not senior enough to be able to bang heads together. Make the objective of the survey somewhat woolly and make sure the manager has to relate to at least three subcommittees plus a panel of union representatives. Add a dash of unsolicited intervention from the chief executive and a change of emphasis half way through…

If the work is delegated to a project team then membership should be representative of the organisation as a whole, and include representation from line management, the union(s) and head office or external specialists. The organisation of the project would look like Figure 4.1.

Fig. 4.1 Organisation of the measurement project

```
┌─────────────────────────────────────────────────────┐
│        ┌────────────────────────────────┐            │
│        │ Measurement team               │            │
│        │ Senior management team         │            │
│        └────────────────────────────────┘            │
│                       │                               │
│                       ▼                               │
│        ┌────────────────────────────────────────┐    │
│        │ Measurement project team               │    │
│        │ Line management representative(s)      │    │
│        │ Employee representative(s)             │    │
│        │ Human resource department representative│   │
│        │ Specialist(s) as necessary             │    │
│        └────────────────────────────────────────┘    │
│                       │                               │
│                       ▼                               │
│        ┌────────────────────────────────┐            │
│        │ Project manager                │            │
│        └────────────────────────────────┘            │
└─────────────────────────────────────────────────────┘
```

The project team should be fully aware of other organisation initiatives planned or in progress in order to create linkages if appropriate and assess their impact on timing.

The team should look at both types of measures – hard and soft. It is not a question of using one or the other – both are needed to create a balanced view.

In the case of soft measures, a typical questionnaire consists of seven parts:

- introductory letter from the senior sponsor;

- a section addressing potential employee concerns;

- definition of wording used;

- the main body of the questionnaire consisting of a series of statement items with associated rating scales;

- an 'additional comments' section;

- a demographics section;

- what to do with the completed questionnaire.

One of the first issues that the project team will need to address is whether to opt for one-way or two-way communication.

COMMUNICATING – ONE-WAY OR TWO-WAY?

Instrument design differs depending on which option is chosen. Both types of instrument consist of items reflecting those aspects of organisational life which affect motivation. But the way the items are presented differs.

One-way communication

Using this approach items are randomly dispersed and are both positively and negatively phrased.

- Example of a positively phrased item:

  'I have confidence in the people I work for.'

- Example of negatively phrased item:

  'We protect our own department before considering the interests of the organisation as a whole.'

The benefit of this approach is that respondents are encouraged to address one item at a time out of context. This approach is popular with those who like to achieve a theoretically less biased answer to each item. The reduced bias is more likely because:

- lack of headings means that the respondent is less sure what overall topic the item is measuring and so he or she responds to the specific meaning of that item alone;

- a mixture of positively and negatively phrased items discourages the respondents from developing a habit of, for example, always ticking a box which represents 'tend to agree';

- random placing of items reduces the bias of fatigue towards the end of the questionnaire.

The box below gives an example of this approach.

Examples of randomly placed items in the BT MNS&S 1998 questionnaire

4 'We build long-term relationships with our customers' (measures delivery).

5 'My work gives me a feeling of personal satisfaction' (measures enjoyment).

6 'Decisions made about employees are usually fair' (measures perception of fairness).

7 'There is a belief in my team that you cannot learn without making mistakes' (measures learning).

Using this approach there is no opportunity to explain within the instrument itself what the senior management team is trying to measure because there are no main headings. There is an opportunity, however, when the results are unscrambled and fed back.

Two-way communication

Using this approach the items, often only positively phrased, are assembled under relevant topic headings. The advantages of this approach are that:

- the headings used can portray the topics seen to be important, and as such communicate the way the senior management team is thinking;

- it is easier for respondents quickly to grasp the meaning of each item and so it is easier and quicker to complete the questionnaire.

The approach runs the risk of respondents developing a habit of answering in a given way, but in practice this is seldom found to happen. People decide for themselves on issues with which they agree or disagree and respond accordingly. The box below gives an example of main headings using this approach.

> **Examples of PricewaterhouseCoopers MCS's main headings 1998**
>
> *Delivering to clients* – we are committed to our clients' success.
> > *Relationships* – We build long-term relationships.
> > *Quality* – We deliver the best in whatever we do.
> > *Results* – We improve clients' business performance.
>
> *Learning* – we get better.
> > *Development* – We develop our professional and knowledge capital.
> > *Creativity* – We develop new products and services, new approaches of doing business.
> > *Challenging* – We question. We value constructive criticism.
>
> *Sharing* – we work as one global team.
> > *Networking* – We share our expertise and experience.
> > *Support* – We help each other develop and deliver work. We help colleagues succeed.
> > *Shared aims* – We follow agreed strategies and plans. Our actions are consistent with those of our colleagues.
>
> *Caring* – we care about each other.
> > *Recognition* – We recognise and reward excellence. We acknowledge and value outstanding work.
> > *Respect* – We build individual and cultural diversity.
> > *Balance* – We seek to balance lifestyle with our global ambition.
>
> *Leading* – we drive our business aggressively.
> > *Leadership* – We establish our direction clearly and visibly. Our beliefs and behaviour are compatible.
> > *Focus* – We are selective in the work we do. We identify and manage risks.
> > *Integrity* – We work to the highest ethical standards.

The main body of the questionnaire contains a series of questions or statements.

DESIGNING THE MAIN BODY

We saw in Chapter 3 that the four contributing organisations created frameworks based on their organisation's value system, business principles or business model.

The main body of the questionnaire contains a series of questions or statements based on the relevant framework to which the respondent is asked to react. The most common are:

- statements (items) with accompanying response scale;
- issues (also items) which are ranked;
- questions soliciting 'free form' answers.

Using statements or items

An example of a statement is: 'My morale is high' to which the respondent is asked to answer, for example, 'yes', 'maybe', 'not sure', 'no', etc.

This approach is incredibly powerful as the measurement team can create a series of statements (items) which reflect the way they judge the organisation should function – in effect defining the preferred 'culture' of the organisation. The resulting ratings from respondents produce a profile of how they view the way the organisation is currently run.

As we will see in Chapter 7 the use of comparison information can help with the interpretation of results. Consequently as the items are being chosen, thought should be given to which organisations, if any, you would like to compare results.

If you are members of a benchmarking club or a salary survey club, for example, it is worth contacting the other members to see if they have a measuring instrument already created, and if so, what items and scales they use. You may not wish to use all of their items, but one or two standardised items in each part of your conceptual framework can be very helpful.

If you prefer not to contact organisations within your own industry then it may be possible, using benchmarking principles, to identify non-competitive organisations with similar operations. For example, Airtours were willing to compare their head office operations with those of insurance companies, and look to compare their front-line staff responses with hotel chains.

The appendix provides examples which you should consider using as core items within your questionnaire.

Using ranked issues

An example of issues to be ranked is shown in Figure 4.2. In this example the ranking is achieved by counting the number of Xs allocated by respondents to each issue. Another way of doing this would be to ask respondents to identify their top three issues and rank them 1 to 3.

This too is a most powerful technique for helping the senior management team to establish priorities on which to focus.

Fig. 4.2   Issues to be ranked

Place an X next to the three issues you think require priority action:	
	(a) Clarity of goals
	(b) Levels of innovation
	(c) Internal communications
	(d) Clarity of organisational structure
	(e) Recognition and reward for good work
	(f) Quality of teamwork
	(g) Relationships between different groups
	(h) Quality of our products and services
	(i) Morale and motivation
	(j) Effectiveness of technology
	(k) Balance between work and personal life
	(l) Effectiveness of learning and education

Using open questions

Examples of the 'open question' approach include the 'targeted' open question and the 'non-specific'.

A targeted open question is often used as a supplementary to a previous statement:

Statement:

We are quick in providing our people with the technology they need.

(Strongly Agree, Agree, etc.)

Targeted open question:

Do you know of anything we can learn from how our competitors use technology?

A non–specific open question is often used as a 'catch all' at the end of the questionnaire. For example:

Please use the space below to add any further comments that would help us understand your views. If you are expanding an answer to a question in the body of the questionnaire, prefix your comments with the question number. Feel free to comment on issues we have not covered. We are very interested to know what works well and what you think could be improved.

In both cases, it is wise to place limits on the length of answer required, otherwise the more verbose respondents will offer an essay as an answer. That is not to say that long answers need to be banned, but such respondents need to be encouraged to organise their thoughts into categories which are then more easily coded and reported. For example:

> As your comments will be typed out into a spreadsheet please restrict each issue to no more than twenty words. If you wish to use more than twenty words send in a separate note.

If the 'one-way' communication option is chosen and the items are randomly dispersed throughout the instrument, they should initially be listed under relevant main headings and then randomised. They can subsequently be realigned to the framework in order to communicate the results.

If the decision is to focus on 'two-way' communication then the items generated can sit under each relevant main heading.

Example from the Airtours Holidays 1997 questionnaire

Under each main heading 10–12 items were listed:

Product quality
'Travel agents describe our holidays accurately.'

Service quality
'Our customers are treated with courtesy.'

Pride in belonging
'Locally Airtours has a good reputation as an employer.'

Resource availability
'I normally have all the information I need to do my job.'

Planning and organisation
'I think work practices in my area are efficient.'

Terms and conditions
'Pay linked to targets tends to discourage cooperation.'

Career development
'People with potential are spotted and developed for the future.'

Standards and targets
'The way my work is measured is fair.'

ADDING CURRENT 'HOT ISSUES'

Although it is possible to create an instrument using a set of standardised items alone, it is important to ensure the current 'hot issues' are included. Otherwise the senior management team runs a greater risk of being seen to be 'out of touch with problems within the organisation'.

There are a number of ways identifying 'hot issues', including:

- focus groups;
- departmental representatives;
- interviews with managers.

The focus groups approach

It is important to ensure the current 'hot issues' are included. Otherwise the senior management team runs a greater risk of being seen to be 'out of touch with problems within the organisation'.

Focus groups consist of a representative range of employees assembled with a group leader to debate and surface the 'hot issues' of the day. If an organisation has already established good 'bottom-up' communication then the issues arising are unlikely to be surprising. But if 'bottom-up' communication has been missing, then assembling focus groups can result in the release of pent up feelings, and as such need to be led sensitively by an experienced facilitator.

Typical outputs from focus groups

Note the range from critical issues to minor complaints.

- Lack of authority to make decisions.
- Making sure everyone understands the mission statement.
- We are always firefighting – not planning enough.
- Timing of departmental meetings needs to be more predictable.
- Effectiveness of meetings in general is poor.
- Not enough ladies' toilets.
- More choice of food in the canteen.
- Customers are unhappy about our speed of reaction.
- People are fighting their corners – not open to criticism.
- Too much waste which can be very costly.
- Office space too cramped.
- Treating people as untrained monkeys.
- Perceived unfairness of internal pay relativity.
- Getting to know about things too late.
- We like being asked – thank you.

The departmental representatives approach

This approach consists of asking each department to nominate their representative who then solicits opinions on what needs to be included in the measuring instrument. The resulting list can either be sent in to the project team or linked to a focus group of representatives.

If appropriate, formal union representatives can be used instead of, or as well as, informally nominated representatives.

Interviews with managers

In most cases managers can be offered their own focus groups, but there may be situations where individual interviews are required. This is particularly important where managerial 'buy in' needs to be sought before the measuring instrument is used. Some of the typical management issues are listed in the box below.

Typical management issues

- Knowing the way people feel about how they are managed.
- Understanding whether xyz is really a problem.
- Do people support what we have been doing over the year?
- Do we have a morale problem in C Division – if so why?
- Is there a feeling that quality of workmanship is deteriorating?
- Are we communicating well enough?
- What do staff think of our new product?
- Is our decision-making seen to be fast enough?
- Are people proud to be associated with our company?
- What do they like/dislike about senior management style?

AVOIDING PITFALLS IN DESIGN

When creating a soft instrument to measure motivation there are a number of pitfalls for the inexperienced. Some of the more common are discussed below.

Using too few items may not capture all of the relevant issues

Consequently the designer misses an opportunity to capture the views of people on the full range of issues.

On the other hand FCP have analysed a 15-item survey for a division of an international oil company. The questionnaire measures one topic – morale. There is a 70% plus response each year, and the instrument meets a limited but specific objective.

Using too many items could result in the instrument being too long

Consequently either the questionnaire is not answered at all, or later answers suffer from response fatigue. Typically each main topic should have 5–7 items. If there are more than this either the topic could be split or there is too much item overlap.

One recent survey that FCP analysed (but did not design) had 140 items and took about 40 minutes to complete. It was clear to the data input team that those items towards the end of the questionnaire were not being answered.

Too many 'open' questions can result in answers that are too long and consequently are costly to capture and analyse

One survey which FCP were asked to analyse consisted of around 50 closed items, each with an open ended equivalent.

Closed question:

The standard of support from the Helpdesk is
1 2 3 4 5
very good – good – adequate – poor – very poor.

Open ended equivalent:

Please comment on your experience of using the Helpdesk:..........................

The open ended items resulted in 3,200 responses of between 10 and 150 words.

Using closed questions requires a choice of scale

Example of a closed item:

I am usually thanked for work well done.	Agree	Tend to agree	Not sure	Tend to disagree	Disagree

Here the response scale can typically range from three to seven. The critical choice is whether to use an even scale where there is no middle or neutral response or an uneven scale (as above) where there is a middle or neutral response.

Practitioners differ in their views on this. Some prefer to encourage a respondent not to 'sit on the fence' and consequently force a 'good – bad' judgement using an even scale. Others take the view that for some issues there can be a legitimate neutral judgement and that 'forcing' can irritate the respondent.

Pragmatically the decision can often be determined by the scale used by comparator organisations with whom you wish to compare results.

Items consist of two or more issues, each one with a different answer

Example of a multi-issue item:

> My pay and benefits are fair for the work I do in this organisation and compared to similar jobs in other organisations.

Here there are four issues rolled into one. The issues are: 1. pay; 2. benefits; 3. compared to other work within the organisation; and 4. compared to similar work outside the organisation.

It is not possible to indicate that benefits are good but pay poor. Nor is it possible to say pay is good in comparison to internal relativities but poor in comparison to external ones.

Items may be phrased ambiguously

Example of an ambiguous item:

> The current reward system motivates me to perform at my best.

On the face of it this has an unambiguous wording. But one organisation in which this was used was in the middle of updating its reward system, and respondents did not know to which system the item was referring. It should have read the 'newly introduced' reward system.

Items may lead the respondents to an obvious answer

Be sure to avoid wording the item in such a way that it 'begs' a given answer.

Example – leading question:

> Would you like a wider range of optional benefits?

Such a question is unlikely to receive many negative answers.

Items can be translated into another language wrongly

It is a good idea to co-opt a specialist in item design onto the measurement team.

Be careful when you need to translate. Make sure that your translation is retranslated back into its original language as a check – otherwise you may experience the embarrassment of one organisation that translated morale as morals (the respondents judged that they had very high morals, but when the translation was corrected, morale was not so high).

Including issues which management will not tackle

If there are issues which management already know are causing concern but which they have no intention of tackling, then careful thought needs to be given whether or not to include items covering the issues. There may still be reasons to include them, for example if management intend to make changes in later years and need a baseline measure of employee attitude, but inclusion needs to be as a result of informed debate.

The use of management speak can be a turn off

Avoid using jargon which non-managerial respondents cannot understand, e.g.

> We are a business with obvious synergies among our specialisations.

As there are so many different pitfalls in designing the range of items it is a good idea to co-opt a specialist in item design onto the measurement team. Often they can be found in a personnel or marketing department. Alternatively use an external specialist agency.

If you prefer to create the items without specialist advice the need for a pilot run of the instrument becomes more critical. If carried out properly it will identify most of the problems above.

ADDING THE SUPPORTING SECTIONS

In developing the draft measurement instrument the team needs to ensure a number of supporting sections are included in the questionnaire before the pilot. The additions should include the following.

Choosing a meaningful name

The instrument needs to be given a name meaningful to all who are planned to receive it:

- Airtours call their survey 'Your Viewpoint'.
- A recent PricewaterhouseCoopers MCS survey was called 'Living our Values'.
- BT MNS&S and Elida Fabergé linked theirs with their change initiatives – 'A Great Place to Work' and 'Listening, Learning, Winning Together'.

Highlighting senior management sponsorship and explanation of context

There needs to be a short introduction from the senior sponsor which includes an explanation of why people are being asked to complete the instrument and what is going to be done with the results. Examples are given below.

Example from BT MNS&S newsletter (linked to their website)

You will have seen the new strategic initiative described on our Homepage. One of these is about making BT MNS&S 'A Great Place to Work'. Quite simply this is about making sure that we focus as much on delighting our people as delighting our customers.

We want BT MNS&S to be an enjoyable and stimulating place. A place where professional expertise is valued, where learning is encouraged, where everyone is able to give of their best, where we share and build on each others' ideas and where people look forward to coming to work...

A Great Place To Work Strategic Initiative.

> **Example from Elida Fabergé (delivered in video form)**
>
> We really believe that learning through people is the only way we can improve the way we work. That is why the title of this year's survey is 'Listening, Learning and Winning Together'. It is important for us to have regular feedback on how you view your job, your company and the conditions in which you work.
>
> I would like each of you to complete a survey questionnaire…this provides us with the strongest base for developing relevant improvement plans for the future…
>
> We will publish the results and then work with you to develop an action plan for improvement.
>
> I will fill in one and so will the management team. I hope all of you will complete one too…
>
> If 85 per cent of you do so the company will say thank you by donating £5,000 to the Give as You Earn (Charity) Committees. I look forward to learning a lot through the feedback.
>
> Keith Weed, Chairman.

Making confidentiality assured

Ensure there is a guarantee of confidentiality signed by the chief executive or equivalent and, if using an independent agency, a repeat guarantee from them. This guarantee goes some way to reducing the fear that individuals will be singled out, and increases the chance that responses will reflect genuine feelings.

> **Example from Airtours Holidays questionnaire**
>
> No one from Airtours will see your reply and we will not report back to Airtours in any way that will single out individuals or small groups of individuals.
>
> Fargus Consulting Partnership.

Defining meanings

Most organisations need to define the wording they are using, particularly if they are different autonomous divisions. Typically these words need defining:

- organisation
- senior management
- manager
- supervisor
- department
- work area
- customer/client
- rewards.

Asking for personal information

When choosing how many ways you want to 'cut' the data there are two conflicting guidelines to bear in mind, both relating to the sensitivities involved in asking for personal information.

The first guideline is to ask for as much information as you are likely to need. You do not subsequently need to analyse all the 'cuts', but you cannot analyse one you have not previously specified.

For example, if you ask people which department they work in, you do not need to separate out the responses into departmental results. But if you do not ask for departmental information, and subsequently decide you should break down the data into departmental responses, you will not be able to do so.

The second guideline is limit your questions to the minimum. This is particularly relevant for first surveys and/or where there are particularly poor employee relations. People are more suspicious of answering a questionnaire with multiple cuts than one with a small number of simple cuts. If you judge your organisation to be in this category, opt for a limited number of demographics in order to maximise trust.

However many demographics you choose it is important to guarantee that subsequent analysis will not be used to identify individuals. As a rule of thumb, groups of below ten people are excluded from any reports, but the number chosen depends on the levels of trust in the organisation. Examples of common demographic data are:

- age range
- division or department

- level of customer contact
- job grade
- length of service
- geographical location
- job title
- recruited from...
- gender
- full time/part time.

Making sure the returns system is clear

Make sure it clear what the respondent has to do next once he or she has completed the instrument.

RUNNING THE PILOT

Before the instrument is printed or made ready for electronic distribution, a pilot run is a must. Some practitioners prefer to use a large pilot, with statistically valid representation. In the case of an organisation with many divisions in many countries, this would be the correct approach.

But in many organisations a pilot does not need to be a long and costly affair. What is needed is a group of 5–10 people from different parts of the organisation to complete the draft document and comment on their experience.

A pilot does not need to be a long and costly affair.

Choose people from different parts of your organisation

The group should include, for example, two employee representatives, one senior line manager, one front-line supervisor, a generalist from the personnel/human resources department and a representative from different main parts of the organisation not already included.

Choose people with a wide range of abilities

Within the group should be at least one very bright individual, one less likely to understand complex items and one who is strongly detail conscious. Most organisations have at least one cynic willing to participate and it is always useful to have his or her comments. Between them the participants should be able to pick up most of the issues discussed in the pitfalls above.

Ask them to time themselves and make notes

During completion they should be asked to time themselves and look out for aspects of the instrument that could affect confidentiality, aspects which are ambiguous and aspects which could be worded better.

Ask for comments

They should highlight aspects of the instrument that they wish to query, and be encouraged to discuss their issues once everyone has finished.

Once the pilot has been completed, and edits made, the finished product should be signed off by the senior sponsor.

PRINTING THE END PRODUCT

The end product may or may not be printed. It is becoming more common to use electronic means for distribution and return (see Chapter 5).

PricewaterhouseCoopers has one of the most sophisticated Lotus Notes applications worldwide. Once their questionnaire is agreed it is integrated into their Notes system and distributed to every partner and employee – either by line of service or by strategic business unit.

Respondents answer the questionnaire and return the completed document to a special unit which immediately logs then deletes the respondent's name. Those that have not responded are sent reminders. The distribution and collection system is paperless.

Nevertheless paper and pencil completion is still the most common approach.

If the questionnaire is to be printed beware of opting for too smart an appearance. Top-quality colour printing runs the risk of people thinking – and commenting – that too much money is being spent.

On the other hand organisations that commonly send out top-quality printed communications should continue to do so in the case of their questionnaire – they cannot afford for it to be seen as a less important document.

KEY POINT SUMMARY

■ Motivation can be measured using both hard and soft measurements. Both should be used, but this book concentrates on the soft approach.

■ The employee survey is the main soft measurement.

■ Before creating a survey instrument it is important to agree its role.

■ Often it is found necessary to set up a measurement team in order to create the instrument and ensure it has support from the decision-makers.

■ A survey instrument can be designed to focus primarily on 'bottom-up' communication, or both ' top-down' and 'bottom-up' communication.

■ It is becoming more common to use standard items so that comparisons between organisations can be made. But before designing your instrument you need to identify the 'hot issues' of the day to ensure they are included.

■ The resulting survey instrument typically consists of seven parts:

   – introductory letter;

   – section addressing employee concerns;

   – definition of wording used;

   – the main body with associated rating scales;

   – an 'additional comments' section;

   – a demographics section;

   – what to do with the completed questionnaire.

■ There are numerous pitfalls to be encountered and it is best to ensure an experienced questionnaire designer is included in the measurement team.

■ Always run a pilot before using a newly created survey instrument.

■ The most common medium for presenting a questionnaire is still 'paper and pencil' but electronic distribution and retrieval is rapidly catching up.

5

Capturing viewpoints

As with the last chapter, only those who are tasked with delivering a survey need read this one. Here we look at the issue of deciding how many of your people to involve.

Once you have your questionnaire created to your satisfaction you need to ensure you capture a 'true' range of opinion. There are two ways an organisation can capture the views of its people: either by tapping the views of a representative sample, or by asking the whole organisation to respond.

DECIDING HOW MANY TO INVOLVE

As a rule of thumb, unless there are good reasons to choose a sampling approach, it is best to involve the whole organisation.

The 'all organisation approach'

The 'all organisation approach' is favoured because:

■ Management want to be seen to involve everyone

> *Our surveys are vitally important in our assessment of how we are progressing towards our goals. I want everyone to have their say and then see that we are listening and actively improving as a result of the feedback we get from the surveys. I'm very much looking forward to the results of Viewpoint 2000.*
>
> Richard Carrick, Managing Director, Airtours Holidays (2000).

■ They want to use the instrument for two-way communication.

> *... You will notice as you complete this questionnaire that it is structured around our new Global Values wheel. Our new wheel reflects the results of last year's survey and sets out the behaviours we must demonstrate throughout MCS to be a world-class player.*
>
> Scott Hartz, Global Managing Partner, PricewaterhouseCoopers MCS (1999).

■ They are using the instrument to generate change.

> *...The results from our last survey provided a foundation for us to develop and improve the business...I will ensure we take action on the results of this survey.*
>
> Peter Rothwell, Managing Director, Airtours Holidays (1995).

■ They have the administrative ability to contact everyone.

> *The response rate to our last survey was an impressive 86%.*
>
> John Sharpe, President, Unilever Home and
> Personal Care – Europe (1998).

But it can be a major administrative task

It is important to appoint a team of people to oversee the administration.

Using the 'all organisation' approach, sending out questionnaires to all staff and keeping track of responses can be an administrative challenge. For this reason, in the case of large multi-site organisations, it is important to appoint a team of people to oversee the administration. Typically the organisation would look as shown in Figure 5.1.

Fig. 5.1 Organisation structure for questionnaire administration

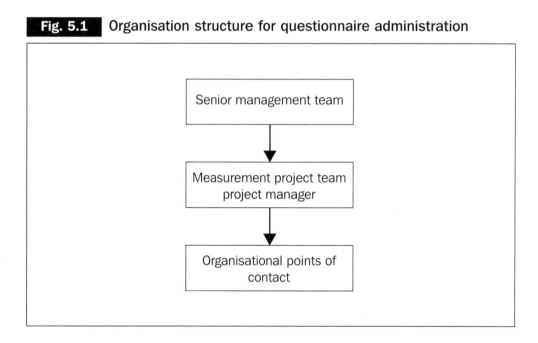

The questionnaires for one large site of a multi-site organisation went missing resulting in the project manager personally photocopying 200 eight page questionnaires in order to meet the agreed schedule. The original boxes of questionnaires were subsequently found resting in the head office mail room.

Typically the team's project manager would be the same person who managed the design of the measurement instrument. He or she would appoint points of contact (PoCs) in all major parts of the organisation.

Points-of-contact role

- Ensure all line managers are aware of the survey and its importance.
- Distribute any pre-survey advertising.
- Ensure all questionnaires are distributed.
- Ensure reminders are well circulated.
- Ensure feedback is received by all.

The PoC should ensure all managers are aware of the survey and its importance, distribute the pre-survey advertising, ensure all questionnaires are distributed, remind people to fill them in and, once the analysis has been carried out, ensure feedback is received.

The sampling approach

Those who opt for a sampling approach do so because:

- Management have used the 'all organisation' approach in the past, and are now monitoring changes in opinion.

  PricewaterhouseCoopers use an 'At A Glance' approach by tapping the opinion of a representative sample of their people.

- They want to achieve a representative range of opinion quickly.

  PricewaterhouseCoopers aims to monitor changes in sentiment quarterly – they can do this only by sampling.

- It is difficult to contact everyone.

  PricewaterhouseCoopers employs 160,000 people worldwide. It is a major administrative task to contact everyone. PricewaterhouseCoopers primarily relies on the 'all organisation' approach, but their 'At A Glance' sampling technique enables a quick snapshot of sentiment when needed.

Sampling by its very nature requires a knowledge of statistics. The objective is to obtain a sample of opinion from a relatively small number of respondents which is representative of the total group being surveyed.

By using sampling techniques, a survey practitioner can obtain a similar result from, say, 10 per cent of the people in the organisation, instead of involving 100 per cent. The catch here is can the practitioner guarantee the results of the sample are similar to the results which would be obtained from the whole?

A practitioner cannot be 100 per cent certain, but using well established statistical techniques the practitioner can say that, for example, s/he can be right

99 times out of 100 that the results from a sample are similar to what would have been achieved from asking the full population.

As a rule of thumb, the smaller the number of people from which you want to take a sample, the larger the percentage of people in the sample needs to be.

When opting for the representative sampling approach it is important to 'catch' close to 100 per cent of the sample selected. If 100 per cent of the sample does not reply, then the sample is less likely to be representative of the whole.

It is for this reason that one vehicle manufacturer gave time off work for all people selected to be in their 10 per cent sample. If anyone could not make their appointment to complete their questionnaire, someone was invited to substitute. By doing this the organisation achieved a 99 per cent response rate from the selected sample.

> For its first employee survey a vehicle manufacturer used its payroll system to create a representative sample. Employees were listed by their employee number (the lowest number represented the longest serving employee, the highest number the newest employee). Then every tenth and eleventh employees were picked. Every tenth person was asked to attend questionnaire completion sessions, with the eleventh acting as substitute in case of absence from work.

USING SURVEY CHAMPIONS

It is useful to appoint local survey champions.

In a large organisation, particularly a multi-site one, it is useful to appoint local survey champions (see Figure 5.2). They can be the same people as the points of contact, but must be well respected senior people. It is their attitude and approach to the survey which will have a major effect on response rates.

Fig. 5.2 Appointment of survey champions

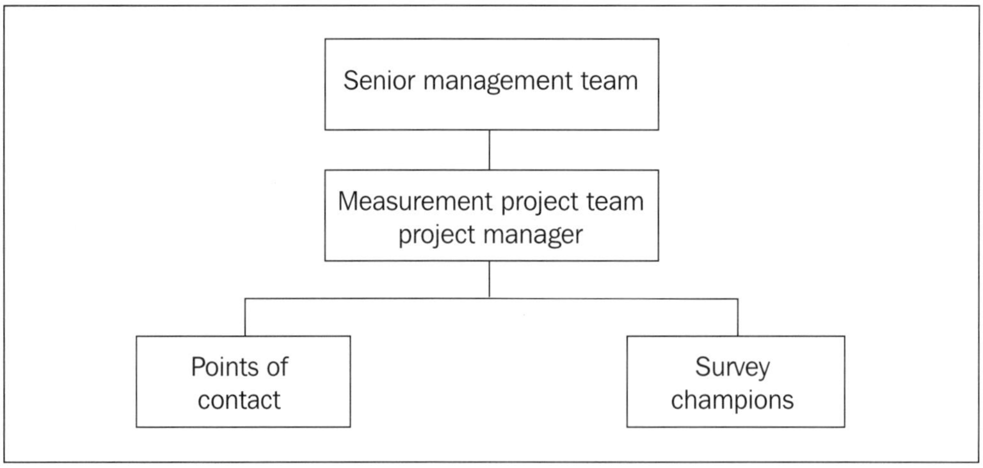

70

DECIDING HOW TO DISTRIBUTE

The hand-completed response to paper-based questionnaires is still the most popular technique for administering a survey. But as new technology becomes accessible to all in an organisation, other options present themselves:

- using basic e-mail;
- using html linked e-mail;
- using web sites.

Using paper-based questionnaires

There are three common means of distributing paper-based questionnaires: group sessions, internal mail and external mail.

Group sessions consist of between 10 and 20 people (but significantly more are possible) who complete the questionnaire in the presence of (usually) an independent administrator. The questionnaires are collected immediately on completion by the administrator.

It is best to use group sessions in order to:

- create a large response in a short time;
- reduce mistrust by using an independent administrator;
- explain face to face why the survey is being carried out;
- help those with reading or language difficulties.

The main drawback is the need to release groups of people from their jobs, although it is possible to reduce this problem by taking only small numbers from each department at any one time.

The *internal mail* approach involves sending the questionnaires out and receiving returns through the organisation's internal mail system. It is best to use this when:

- people are used to completing questionnaires;
- a good level of trust has been established;
- the internal communications system is reliable;
- it is feasible for departments to collect and send back their own returns in bulk.

The main drawback of this approach is the perceived (and maybe actual) lack of confidentiality.

The *external mail* approach normally still uses internal mail to distribute the questionnaires, but the responses are returned individually to an external agency. This is best used when trust has not yet been established.

The two main drawbacks are the postal costs and the difficulty in keeping track of responses. However, the use of an efficient external agency can ensure that tracking is possible by providing a cumulative count of responses by department.

Using electronic questionnaires

There are three main types of electronic questionnaire: basic e-mail, html enhanced e-mail and web site.

Basic e-mail is one possible system of delivery

At the crudest level it is possible to create a basic questionnaire using a standard e-mail system and distribute it to all people on your system. The questionnaire is written as part of the text of the e-mail. Respondents click on the 'return to sender' option and enter an 'X' or type their reply into boxes with square brackets [ ] to indicate their responses.

There are difficulties with this approach, however:

- the questionnaire can look amateurish;
- it is not possible to specify a route through the questions;
- it is not possible to constrain the responses;
- respondents can return multiple responses if they are so minded;
- it is possible to identify the responder because his or her address is attached to the reply.

Basic e-mail systems do not allow for sophisticated questionnaire design, nor routing the respondent past questions that are irrelevant to them. Also, respondents can (and do) change the meaning of the questions to suit their answers, or offer a mini thesis as a response to the issues causing the most concern.

There are ways of resolving the possibility of multiple responses and respondent identification technically, but the last issue does require a high level of trust from respondents – or responses need to be sent directly to an independent agency.

Html linked e-mail is a better proposition

Using hyper text mark-up language (html) it is possible to create a professional-looking questionnaire which enables the responses to be constrained and allows for the respondent to be guided to the questions which are most relevant, based on his or her pattern of initial responses.

For surveys that need to be translated into numerous languages, the use of electronic distribution is a big plus. The questionnaire still needs to be correctly translated, of course, but it is possible for each respondent to choose in which language he or she would like to complete the questionnaire simply by pressing a button.

The finished questionnaire can be attached to an e-mail system and distributed. On receipt, if the system is set up correctly, an html browser (e.g. Microsoft Explorer or Netscape Navigator) is loaded and shows the questionnaire ready for completion.

The problems of multiple responses and respondent identification still remain but, as above, the risks can be reduced technically.

Intranet web sites

Intranet *web sites* are another possible way of delivering the instrument. In this case the questionnaire resides on the web site and respondents are alerted to its existence both by e-mail and by traditional communication methods.

To ensure that each respondent gives only one response a login system may be employed. For example, the respondent follows the e-mailed link to a web page which asks them for their login (and possibly password) identity.

Once the questionnaire is completed within the site it is ready for distribution to, or collection by, the survey administrator.

Temporary web sites can also be employed for the duration of the survey if the organisation does not have its own. Many of the independent agencies can provide this service.

Respondents' replies are either stored centrally on the internet or intranet web server (from where they may be downloaded for analysis) or they may be e-mailed to the receiver. In either case, respondents' replies are imported into a suitable program for analysis.

Each of the proprietary systems available has its own methodology so it is necessary to design the questionnaire, publish it and recover responses using the same system. From that point, the same system may provide analysis facilities or it may be necessary to use another system for data analysis.

Questions to ask of your IT department

- Do potential respondents have easy access to e-mail?

- Do potential respondents have their own (unshared) e-mail address?

- Do potential respondents have access to an intranet or the internet?

- Can we create questionnaire using html?

- Can our e-mail system deliver html-based documents?

- Do we carry out enough surveys to merit the purchase of a suitable all-in-one system for conducting web and e-mail surveys?

ENSURING A RESPECTABLE RESPONSE

By following the steps set out in this book so far readers will have gone a long way to ensuring a good response to their survey.

The 'goodness' of response depends on whether a census or a sample of employees is chosen. As explained above, a representative sample needs close to 100 per cent response or it will not remain representative.

If all people are asked to complete the instrument, then experience suggests that the minimum response rate that most organisations aim for is 50 per cent. Although statistically a much lower figure is theoretically acceptable, most management teams feel that a response of less than 50 per cent does, in itself, underline the message that motivation is low.

As a rule of thumb a 'good' response from a census approach is 60–70 per cent, with over 70 per cent being particularly good. Ways to help achieve a respectable response include:

- *Active involvement of the chief executive.* If respondents believe that their ratings and comments will be seen (without censorship) at senior management levels, then they are more likely to respond. Consequently the more the chief executive (or equivalent) can ensure people know he or she is actively interested in the results the better.

- *Active management support.* There is a definite link between the attitude of a line manager and the number of responses from his or her team. Consequently make sure all line managers are well briefed and convinced before the distribution.

- *Union involvement.* If there is formal union representation, make sure they are involved either in the project team or when surfacing 'hot topics', or both.

- *Pre-distribution advertising.* Make sure that people are expecting their questionnaires, understand the reason for them and know what will be done with them. Emphasise confidentiality.

- *Ensuring people understand why.* If respondents understand why the instrument is being used – for example, as a way of collecting people's views prior to agreeing the annual business plan – then the more they will be inclined to respond.

- *Promise of action.* Measurement without action is a sin. If people are to invest their time in answering the questionnaire then they need to be assured that the senior management team will take note of the results and act on them (or explain why immediate action will not be taken).

- *Follow-up from the last survey.* One of the reasons that measurement without action is a sin is that if no action is taken as a result of one survey, then fewer people will be disposed to respond to the next. Make sure people know what has happened as a result of the last survey. Good 'internal public relations' is a must.

■ *Donations to charity.* Consider making a donation to charity for each questionnaire completed. If your organisation is associated with a specific charity so much the better.

■ *Timing.* Where feasible organise the distribution outside of key holiday periods and heavier than normal workloads.

■ *Completion 'in work'.* Enable people to complete their questionnaire in work. For example, if you operate regular briefing groups, encourage questionnaire completion during the brief.

■ *Controlling returns.* Establish a system of logging in returns, preferably including the facility for identifying which part of the organisation they are coming from. By doing this it is possible to 'chase' responses from low responding departments.

■ *Electronic reminders.* In the case of electronically distributed questionnaires it is possible to send auto-reminders to participants who have not returned their survey. These can significantly boost the returns, particularly if the reminder is timed to coincide with less busy periods in the week.

KEY POINT SUMMARY

■ In capturing the views of your employees, you can either take a representative sample or ask the whole organisation to respond.

■ The 'all organisation' approach is chosen when:

　– the senior management team wants to involve everyone;

　– the instrument is designed to communicate 'top down' as well as 'bottom up';

　– the instrument is being used to generate planned change;

　– it is administratively possible to contact everyone.

■ The 'sampling' approach is chosen when:

　– the 'all organisation' option has been used and the senior management team wants to monitor changes of opinion;

　– a representative range of opinion needs to be tapped quickly;

　– it is difficult to contact everyone.

■ In large organisations it is important to appoint survey champions and points of contact.

- Distribution can be by 'snail mail' or e-mail, or via web sites.
- There are numerous ways of helping to achieve a respectable response, including pre-survey internal marketing, the active involvement of the senior management team, active union support, active management support and the promise of subsequent action.

Making data meaningful

In previous chapters we discussed the importance of measuring motivation, how it should fit in with a battery of measures, how to develop soft measures, and how to capture viewpoints.

This chapter too need be read only by those tasked with delivering a survey. It looks at the stage where data streaming in from throughout an organisation is consolidated and transformed into meaningful information.

Many organisations use external agencies to do this as it requires a range of capabilities less likely to be found internally or, more likely, in great demand internally. These capabilities include:

- maintaining confidentiality;

- consolidating individual responses;

- categorising;

- controlling data quality;

- describing the results.

The only capability listed above which may be difficult to achieve in-house is that of generating trust so that that confidentiality will be respected. Particularly in the case of a first survey, respondents will seldom believe that internal analysis can remain confidential.

> Respondents will seldom believe that internal analysis can remain confidential.

The critical resource necessary to carry out the measurement in-house is the necessary software together with an analyst experienced in the use of that software. Nowadays there is plenty of software available on the open market. For example:

- Survey Analysis Package (SNAP) by Mercator Computer Systems;

and for smaller surveys:

- Microsoft Office Access and/or Excel.

But for organisations without existing capability or, more commonly, with existing capability overstretched, the external agency route is a credible alternative.

We will look at the capabilities one at a time.

MAINTAINING CONFIDENTIALITY

Potential issues of confidentiality include completed questionnaires being traced to their respondents and handwriting used for written comments being recognised. It has also been known for comments to contain specific examples which give away the identity of the respondent.

And the more demographic data that is requested in the questionnaire the more suspicious people will be. (How many female supervisors aged between 40 and 50 in the maintenance section can there be?).

A respondent to one survey was concerned about the 'tracing system' used to identify where the completed questionnaires had come from, and mentioned this in his comments section. The 'tracing system' turned out to be the stationer's reorder number which was, of course, the same on all envelopes.

Organisations that have successfully used surveys for some time find that initial suspicions reduce significantly, but it only takes one slip to reintroduce the fear of being singled out. The rule of thumb is to tread very carefully.

CONSOLIDATING INDIVIDUAL RESPONSES

The most common means of response consolidation is linked to the most common method of distribution – manual data input from a paper questionnaire completed by hand.

Other ways which are challenging manual input are:

- *Scanning*. This is most useful when the questionnaire consists of one or two sides of closed questions, together with a rating scale. The questionnaire is completed by hand and returned to a central point. The responses are stacked onto an automatic feeder and then rapidly fed onto the scanner bed. The scanner scans in the responses and these are stored in a file. The data can subsequently be exported into standard analysis software. The process is akin to that used by the National Lottery.

  One disadvantage of this method is that not all scanners can read handwritten comments. Those that can require large amounts of disk space and do not always interpret the handwriting correctly.

- *E-mail*. The completed questionnaires are sent back to the survey administrator and downloaded into a database. Then, depending on the system used, they can be read immediately as a database or downloaded into one. Any free format answers can normally be exported into appropriate software for subsequent coding and analysis.

- *Web sites*. Once the respondent has completed the questionnaire, answers can automatically be captured and one of two options follow. Either the analysis software resides on the web site and an analysis of the responses can be carried out 'live', or the responses are e-mailed to the survey administrator for subsequent analysis.

  As intranets become more established this form of data capture will become one of the more popular approaches. This is because the senior management team can ask fewer questions more often, so capturing a snapshot of people's views to a range of 'hot issues' as they develop.

Questions to ask your IT Department

- If using e-mail, is it possible to delete respondents' identification automatically on receipt of their answer?
- Can we minimise the likelihood of multiple responses from the same person?
- Is it likely that our server will be overwhelmed by respondents?
- Is it possible to target reminder notes to those individuals who have not yet responded?

CATEGORISING FREE-FORMAT ANSWERS

If you have opted to use even one open question, the free-format answers will need to be captured and analysed. If the response is based on paper and pencil then the responses will also need to be typed before they can be categorised. Electronic responses are less onerous as they are input automatically by the respondents.

A common way of capturing and analysing the responses is to use a spreadsheet. Each comment is either typed or imported into a column of cells and then categorised by using a code in the neighbouring cells. The categories can then be grouped easily using the 'sort' function of the spreadsheet.

An example of comments relating to pay is given in Table 6.1.

Table 6.1 Examples of free-format answers relating to pay

Category	Comment
Pay	Bureaucratic salary structure – inflexible, unrewarding and low.
Pay	The flexible benefits cost too much and erode my salary.
Pay	People should be paid broadly similar amounts for doing similar jobs within the same department and between departments.
Pay	In general salary/bonus rates are too low to reward staff for their efforts.
Pay	On various occasions I have been told by my manager that because I am on a high salary I am not eligible for a pay rise.
Pay	The worst thing about the company is the perceived level of pay differences between people doing the same job.
Pay	Lack of transparency and consistency in terms of internal procedure, e.g. salary bands, appraisals, etc.

The problems encountered in effecting a classification are, firstly, what categories to use, and then ensuring that similar comments are consistently placed under the same category.

Recent developments in software provide a second way of categorising the comments. Once correctly programmed the software can classify each comment it analyses according to the wording used by the respondent. The analysis needs to be tested and reclassified depending on how many words the program has misinterpreted. For example the word 'file' can be classified under 'information technology' or 'office' depending on the context.

An example of the range of themes found in one survey can be seen in Table 6.2, together with some of the 'alias' words which the software was programmed to include within the categories.

Recent developments in software provide a second way of categorising the comments.

Table 6.2 Classification and alias

1. Accommodation	Files, chairs, desks, filing cabinet, office space.
2. Agility	Alert, market, marketplace, flexible, speed, quick, quickly.
3. Excellence	World-beating, world-class, world-leading, excellent, expert, expertise.
4. Informed	Communicate, communications, e, e-mail, meeting, meetings, newsletter, newsletters.
5. Innovation	Creative, solutions, new, ideas, improve.
6. IT	Internet, portables, technology, database, computer, laptop, equipment, PC, software, helpline, infrastructure.
7. Leadership	Leader, style, management, guidance, direction, vision, goals, strategy, lead, led, leading, leader's.
8. Learning	Training, education, course, study, knowledge, exams, development, opportunity, coaching, counselling, guidance, subject matter, secondments.
9. Morale	Happy, dissatisfied, demoralising, demoralised, atmosphere, spirit, feel.
10. Recognition	Reward, perform, performance, compensation, salary, pay, promotion, money, appraisal, review, appreciated, evaluation forms.
11. Respect	Contributions, involvement, contribution, value, valued, nationality, religion, age, gender, disability, support, discrimination, equal.
12. Support staff	Support, switchboard, administration, secretary, secretarial.
13. Survey	Thanks, circulation, questionnaire.
14. Trust	Consistent, inconsistent, fair, fairness, honest, honesty, dishonest, dishonesty.
15. Teamwork	Team cooperation, competition, confrontational, teams', teams, co-operate, cooperate, co-operation, relationship, share, sharing, open, trusting, trust, debriefing.
16. Work-life	Pressure, stress, overtime, life, home, weekends, weekend, family, flexible working.

Once classified it is possible to 'measure' the level of interest using a simple count or a count expressed as a percentage of the total.

The comments, once linked to the ratings received for the main body of the questionnaire, can become a very powerful qualitative accompaniment to the statistics. Chapter 2 offers some examples of comments received.

CONTROLLING DATA QUALITY

On a more mundane level it is important to pay attention to quality control. This relates to the following.

Searching out dud responses

Some responses are 'dud' because the respondent has not completed the questionnaire properly. Reasons for this range from mischief to boredom, misunderstanding to fatigue.

Capturing data accurately

As explained above, data capture can be based on physical data entry or scanning and electronic means. The accuracy of the data capture must be guaranteed before the end results can be accepted.

Transferring data accurately between different pieces of software

Theoretically there should be no need to use more than one piece of software. For example, answers provided through the 'web' option can be transformed into readable data by the same piece of software. Also, there are suites of software that now both analyse data and present the results graphically.

However, it is possible that data will need to be transferred because the analysis is carried out on software different from that of the subsequent presentation. An example is transferring responses from Lotus Notes database to a more powerful statistical package such as SNAP, or the analysis may be in Microsoft Access and the subsequent presentation may be in Microsoft PowerPoint.

If data is transferred, time needs to be allocated to ensure that data reappears in the correct format.

Reporting the results of negatively worded items

This is a simple problem, but it can become tortuous. If a decision has been made to use negatively phrased items, then a policy decision needs to be made as to how to report back on the results.

- Option one is to reverse the polarity of the scale so that all favourable answers are at the same pole.

- Option two is to keep the polarity different, but present all favourable results in one colour and unfavourable in another.

DESCRIBING THE RESULTS

The main objective at this stage in the process is to compact the responses from (usually) hundreds, if not thousands, of people into patterns from which trends and themes can be spotted. In order to do this there are two common measuring techniques and two common presentation techniques.

Common measuring techniques

The two common measuring techniques are:

- percentage of responses;

- average score.

Table 6.3 demonstrates the *'percentage favourable' approach*. This way of compacting the response to a readily understandable figure adds together all the favourable scores to provide an overall 'percentage favourable' score. In this case the 'percentage favourable' is 70 per cent (10 + 60).

Table 6.3 'Percentage favourable' approach

	Agree	Tend to agree	Not sure	Tend to disagree	Disagree
Our manager holds team briefings every week	10	60	5	20	5

The advantages of the approach are:

- most people understand the measure;

- differences in scores for one year to the next are immediately meaningful.

The disadvantage of this approach is that it excludes some of the information on the scale. A low 'percentage favourable' score could be due to a high 'not sure' or high 'percentage unfavourable' and unless the whole scale is presented this is unknown.

The second approach is to convert the scale into an *average score*. The average is obtained by applying a value to the 'agree', 'tend to agree', etc. positions on the scale, and then making the calculation. In Table 6.4 the responses have been allocated a value of 2 to −2, and consequently the average score would be 0.5, that is

$$[(2 \times 10) + (1 \times 60) + (0 \times 5) + (-1 \times 20) + (-2 \times 5)] / 100 = 0.5$$

Table 6.4 Average score

	Agree	Tend to agree	Not sure	Tend to disagree	Disagree
Value of 2 to −2	2	1	0	−1	−2
Our manager holds team briefings every week	10	60	5	20	5

In Table 6.5 the values allocated are 1–5, and consequently the average score is 2.5:

$$[(1 \times 10) + (2 \times 60) + (3 \times 5) + (4 \times 20) + (5 \times 5)] / 100 = 2.5$$

Table 6.5 Average score

	Agree	Tend to agree	Not sure	Tend to disagree	Disagree
Value of 1 to 5	1	2	3	4	5
Our manager holds team briefings every week	10	60	5	20	5

The average therefore will depend on the value given to each part of the rating scale. The choice is simply a matter of personal preference.

Presentation techniques

The common presentation techniques are:

■ spreadsheets;

■ column and bar charts;

■ pie charts.

Spreadsheets are often the first step to be used when analysing data. Information can be condensed to give a summary of responses received by, for example, business unit. In Figure 6.1 the base figure is the overall response rate in 'absolute' figures.

Fig. 6.1   Example of spreadsheet layout

People are proud to belong to this company

	All	Area 1	Area 2	Area 3	Unit 1	Unit 2	Unit 3	Unit 4	Unit 5
Base	7019	2016	3709	1294	165	11	64	54	25
Disagree	3	4	2	6	7	0	6	11	4
Neither	12	14	9	18	15	0	17	13	20
Agree	83	81	88	74	78	100	77	74	76

The remaining figures are the percentage response for all 'disagree' responses, all 'neither' responses and all 'agree' responses. Where figures do not add up to 100 per cent it is because the 'no response' figure has been left out.

Here we have what looks to be an overall good result. Even if we were to compare it to 'best in class' data and it shows that improvements are possible, the 'all organisation' figure of 83 per cent may well suggest to the senior management team that other issues are of higher priority. At the same time it is worth noting that there is some variation in the results which may be statistically significant (see Chapter 7).

Column or *bar charts* are a good way of presenting the percentage favourable (or average) scores because differences are easily demonstrated and comparisons easily made. An example column chart is shown in Figure 6.2.

Fig. 6.2   Example of a column chart

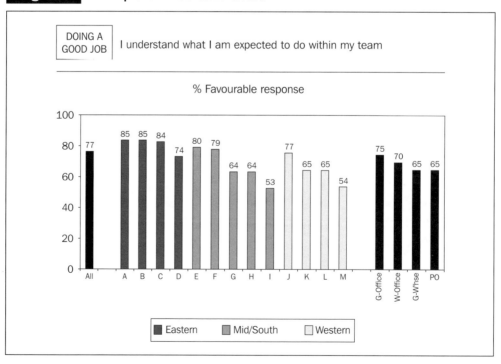

In this case the overall organisation result is shown on the left, and the results for different business units and departments within each unit are spread over the chart. The presentation highlights what is possible in terms of 'understanding what I am expected to do', and provides an internal 'best in class' example to which others can aspire.

Pie charts are equally good for presenting results, but less can be placed on a page when compared to bar charts and this has implications for presentations to senior management. In the example shown in Figure 6.3 the range of comments received have been classified and the percentage in each category presented.

Fig. 6.3   Example of a pie chart

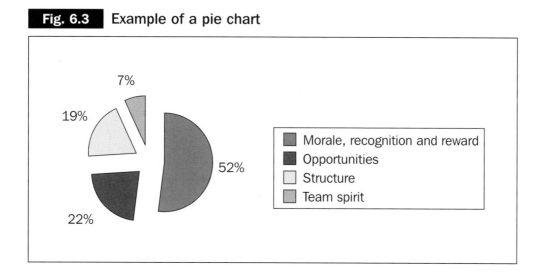

Once an easily understandable measure and presentation have been established the search for trends and themes can commence.

KEY POINT SUMMARY

- The critical factors required for making data meaningful are:
  - generating trust that individual results will be kept confidential;
  - availability of suitable software and an experienced analyst;
  - ability to classify information consistently;
  - attention to detail when exercising quality control;
  - a simple way of describing the results.

- Often internal capability is either non-existent or overstretched, and the use of external agencies is common.

- The data received should be presented using easy-to-read charts which demonstrate trends and themes.

7

Searching for trends and themes

This is the last chapter the deliverer of surveys needs to read alone – Chapter 8 onwards is common ground for all the senior management team.

The search for trends and themes ranges from the application of basic common sense to the application of statistical techniques. Those on low budgets usually stick to common sense.

USING COMMON SENSE

Many senior management teams' organisations find the 'common-sense' analysis enough to spot trends and themes because the management team already suspect they exist and it is just a question of establishing a measurement.

The common-sense approach uses spreadsheets and bar charts to identify, for example, what people see as the main priorities on which to focus. The chart shown in Figure 7.1 is a case in point.

Fig. 7.1 Bar chart to identify priorities

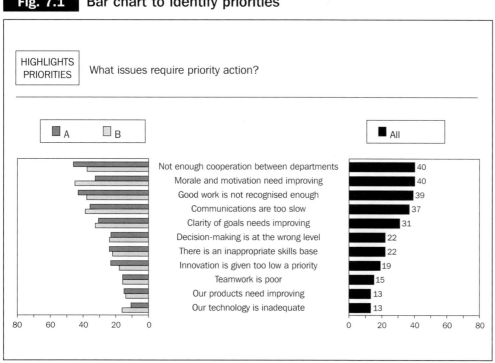

In the figure the bars on the right represent the 'all-organisation' score and the bars on the left two different business units. When reviewing the results the management team may well decide to concentrate their efforts on:

- identifying ways to improve cross-department cooperation;
- what might be done to improve motivation;
- improving ways of recognising effort and results.

Another simple approach to analysis is to spot regular deviations from the 'all-organisation' score or the 'internal best in class' score. In the spreadsheet shown in Figure 7.2 a quick look at the percentage favourable scores shows team 4 to be scoring generally less favourably than the 'all-organisation' score. Also team 2 appears to have 'got it together' better than the rest. The averaging of the scores at the bottom of the spreadsheet also provides a pointer to the differences between the teams.

Fig. 7.2 Spreadsheet approach identifies deviations from the norm

	Percentage Favourable Scores					
	All %	Team 2 %	Team 3 %	Team 4 %	Team 5 %	Team 7 %
I feel the company is a good employer	61	78	63	54	47	50
Normally when I go home I feel I have achieved something useful	72	89	68	54	65	79
People I work with cooperate to get the job done	86	89	100	92	88	89
I am usually able to influence decisions affecting work in my team	64	89	84	38	65	64
Decision-making is made at the right level	42	44	42	23	47	43
I have enough authority to do my job well	74	67	84	85	76	71
I feel I am 'kept in the know' about what is happening within the company	61	78	53	62	53	61
In my team people are encouraged to be open and trusting	69	89	79	62	65	79
We are encouraged to speak our minds	61	89	74	38	82	54
The building I work in is suitable for our business needs	55	78	32	62	47	96
The organisation provides me with effective education and training	61	78	63	38	76	54
My manager devotes sufficient time to coaching team members	45	44	37	15	65	43
I am usually thanked for work well done	70	89	68	54	76	71
I feel my contribution is valued by the organisation	48	67	58	38	41	43
My job enables me to use my skills and abilities to the full	68	78	68	54	82	71
Average percentage for all items	62	76	65	51	65	65

Next, using the full range of scores, it is often worth highlighting those which have a high 'not sure' score. This can be important as it can demonstrate a lack of knowledge/understanding and/or a possible gap in communication or training. The spreadsheet in Figure 7.3 demonstrates this point.

Fig. 7.3   Use of a spreadsheet to identify possible gaps in knowledge

Planning and Organisation

Q45   Our organisation has a well defined business plan

	All	Cut1	Cut2	Cut3	Cut4	Cut5	Cut6
	235	27	22	33	17	21	10
Agree	14	11	0	9	24	14	20
Tend to agree	16	4	14	24	29	29	30
Not sure	**51**	**48**	**77**	**45**	**29**	**38**	**50**
Tend to disagree	5	11	9	9	6	5	0
Disagree	3	4	0	3	6	10	0

Q46   My department/team has a well defined business plan

	All	Cut1	Cut2	Cut3	Cut4	Cut5	Cut6
	235	27	22	33	17	21	10
Agree	17	11	9	6	35	14	10
Tend to agree	25	4	41	48	24	38	20
Not sure	**37**	**41**	**45**	**33**	**29**	**14**	**60**
Tend to disagree	4	7	5	3	0	5	0
Disagree	6	15	0	0	6	19	0

Q47   Our training activities link effectively with our business plan

	All	Cut1	Cut2	Cut3	Cut4	Cut5	Cut6
	235	27	22	33	17	21	10
Agree	8	7	0	6	0	5	10
Tend to agree	17	11	18	12	24	33	10
Not sure	**47**	**44**	**59**	**61**	**59**	**24**	**70**
Tend to disagree	8	11	18	9	0	5	0
Disagree	7	7	5	3	6	14	0

Q48   Our training resources are normally able to meet the needs of planned training activities

	All	Cut1	Cut2	Cut3	Cut4	Cut5	Cut6
	235	27	22	33	17	21	10
Agree	15	11	23	12	12	10	20
Tend to agree	30	44	36	42	24	29	20
Not sure	**31**	**26**	**23**	**27**	**47**	**24**	**30**
Tend to disagree	4	0	9	0	0	5	10
Disagree	6	0	5	3	0	14	0

In the spreadsheet there are too many 'not sure' scores (shown in bold italics) to be comfortable. It could be argued that non-managers would be less likely to be able to comment on the issues outlined, but in a well-run organisation people who feel involved would normally have a view.

Where results for a few years are available, bar or column charts are useful for highlighting changes in sentiment. In the example shown in Figure 7.4 there are three business units which have measured motivation over a period of five years, and one over four. Each BU shows a generally upward trend.

Fig. 7.4 Use of a column chart to highlight changes over time

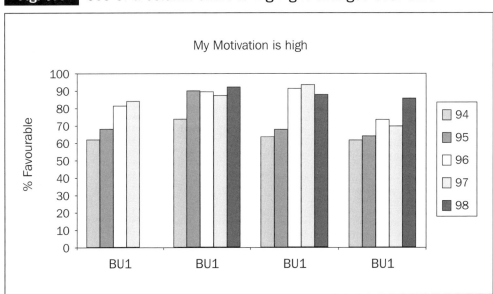

Lastly, combinations of item scores can be related to an organisation model. By doing this the priorities can be seen in the context of the operating model/values on which the survey is based.

Fig. 7.5 Use of BQF Business Excellence Model

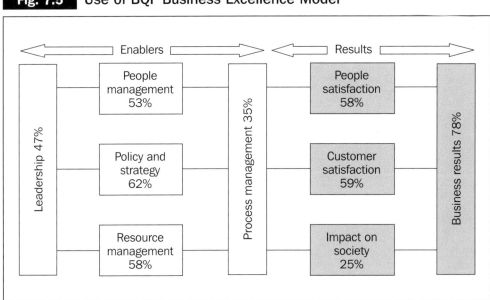

In the BQF Business Excellence Model shown in Figure 7.5 the percentages shown represent the average percentage favourable scores for the clusters of items used. It can be seen that the process management (representing the efficiency of the organisation) would probably be a prime target for improvement activity. Management may also decide to review their policy towards the various aspects of 'impact on society'.

USING EXTERNAL COMPARISONS

If the senior management team is interested in comparing results with other organisations, then this aspect should have been discussed during the instrument design stage (see Chapter 4). The design should incorporate question/item wording which is close to that used by the comparators.

The appendix at the end of the book provides examples which you should consider using as core items in your questionnaire.

It is becoming more commonplace for organisations to want to 'benchmark' against others, and benchmarking clubs are developing quickly. The clubs organised by independent survey agencies or organisations with common interests are designed to enable comparisons such as:

> It is becoming more commonplace for organisations to want to 'benchmark' against others.

- by industry, e.g. fast-moving consumer goods, professional services;

- by country, e.g. UK, USA, Germany, Japan;

- by success, e.g. high performing organisations;

- by business cycle, e.g. in transition, high/low morale, in trauma.

Making valid comparisons

Effecting a valid comparison can be a tricky business which involves ensuring the following:

- *The wording has the same meaning.* For example, 'my morale is high' and 'morale in my department is high' do not mean the same thing and generate different answers.

- *The workforce has similar characteristics.* For example, comparing head office staff in Airtours and Elida Fabergé may be valid but comparing factory employees with holiday representatives probably will not be.

- *The scales used are the same.* For example, comparing the results of a five- and seven-part scale may be possible (although some practitioners would not be willing to do this) but comparing the results of a five- and six-point scale would not be valid (because the five-point scale has a middle point and the six-point scale forces a response one way or the other).

Comparisons, when they are valid, can, however, be very useful, enabling the senior management team to draw comfort from 'less favourable' scoring, or realise that their 'favourable' scores are not actually that good.

The primary focus should be on the internal information.

However, a word of warning: the primary focus should be on the internal information. Members of the senior management team should be asking themselves 'are we satisfied with the fact that 80 per cent of our people understand how their objectives contribute to the business plan?' (What about the 20 per cent that didn't?) The indication that most other organisations achieve a less favourable score should not, in itself, result in complacency.

From the surveys in which the author has been involved it is possible to offer the score ranges shown in Table 7.1.

Table 7.1   What employees think: examples of high and low scores

	Low per cent favourable score %	High per cent favourable score %
How senior managers behave Items relating to creating a clear vision	40	76
How people are managed Items relating to a climate of support and trust	43	90
How efficient the organisation is Items relating to how well their business is organised	14	71
How resources are managed Items relating to the provision of resources necessary to do the job	25	71
Reputation and success Items relating to quality of products/services	25	85

USING STATISTICAL TECHNIQUES

The use of statistics requires a specialist to help determine what formulae to use and what the results mean. The statistical techniques most commonly used are:

- those enabling management to know whether differences in results are 'real' or simply due to random occurrences (tests of significance);
- those enabling management to establish a close relationship between two sets of figures (correlation);

- those enabling causal relationships to be established (regression);
- those which sort your results into groupings based on similarity of responses (cluster or factor analysis).

These are covered below. For readers who are not interested in this aspect of survey technology, move on to Chapter 8. Readers who are will find a basic explanation below, but not the warnings about obtaining professional advice – there are many factors to be taken into consideration when opting for the statistical route.

Real differences or not?

There are three main types of differences in which the senior management team are likely to be interested.

Differences between different organisational 'cuts'

During the design of the measuring instrument there will have been discussions concerning what demographic questions to include, for example department/business unit, job grade, gender, age, etc. A list of typical demographic data can be found in Chapter 4. The analysis of the data will have produced a spreadsheet or bar chart which indicates differences in scoring between, for example, two different divisions (see Figure 7.6).

Fig. 7.6 Divisional differences in scoring

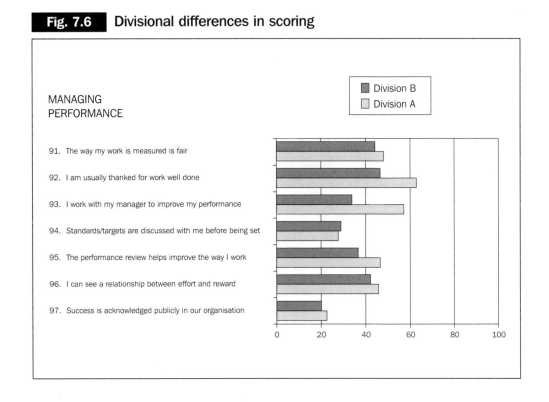

In Figure 7.6, management may be willing to accept the differences between divisions for items 92 and 93 as being 'true' differences (that is, not by chance). But what about items 94, 95, 96 and 97? A statistical test will provide a better indicator as to whether the difference is 'true' or not, but even using such a test, it is still not possible to be 100 per cent certain.

Differences between two different survey results

When surveys are used to track changes in motivation over time the analysis will have compared results for specific items or groups of items from one survey to the next.

In the example shown in Figure 7.7, management may be willing to accept that the increase in pride for every cut is not due to chance. But, as before, using a statistical test would indicate how likely it is that the differences are 'real'.

Fig. 7.7 Tracking changes over time

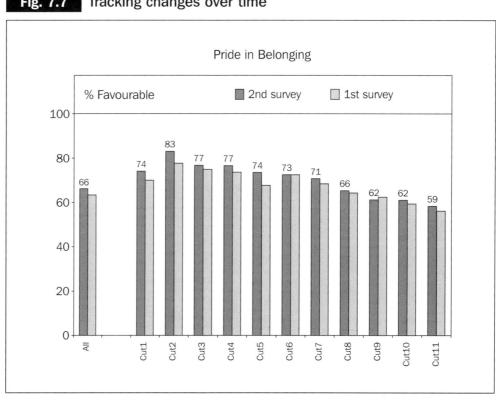

Difference between your organisation and a comparator

If you decide to compare your results with those of another organisation or group of organisations, then you will need to know if apparent differences are true or more likely to be by chance.

In the example shown in Figure 7.8, the extreme differences may be taken as 'true', but in the case of the smaller differences in the middle, only a statistical test will suffice.

Accordingly, in many cases management may wish to subject the data to a statistical analysis in order to provide a way of determining the probability of a difference being true or due to chance.

Fig. 7.8 Differences in scores between two organisations

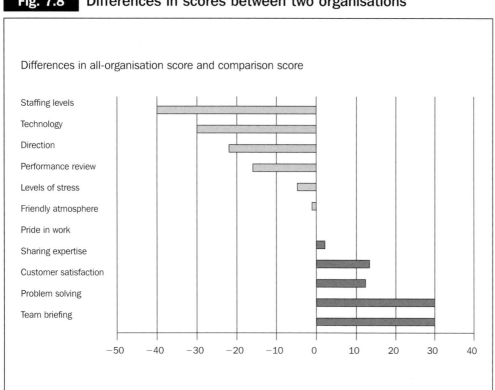

Finding the relationship between two sets of data

There are occasions when the senior management team would like measure the relationship between two sets of information created as part of the survey. This approach is called correlation.

For example, the senior management team might want to establish whether or not there is a relationship between survey results and productivity or customer satisfaction. The two sets of data might look like Table 7.2. The relationship can also be visualised. In the case of the data in Table 7.2, the graph would look like Figure 7.9 (in practice the relationship is likely to be less obvious).

Table 7.2 Survey data

Business unit	% favourable score from employee survey	% satisfied score from customer survey
1	62	80
2	60	50
3	82	85
4	74	69
5	47	57
6	75	60
7	87	90
8	65	73
9	59	63
10	40	35

Fig. 7.9 Graph of survey data

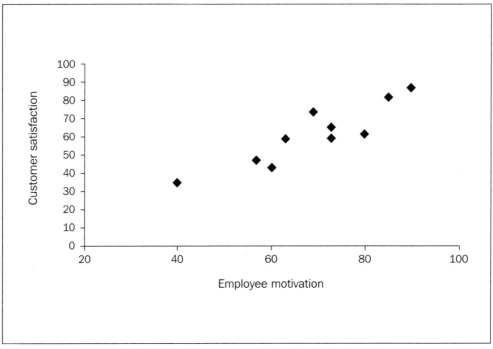

The relationship between the two sets of figures can also be expressed numerically, ranging from −1 to 1, with 0 representing no linear relationship and 1 representing a perfect linear relationship. The relationship for the data used in Figure 7.9 would be expressed as 0.78. If there were little or no relationship the graph would look like Figure 7.10.

Fig. 7.10 Graph showing no relationship between data

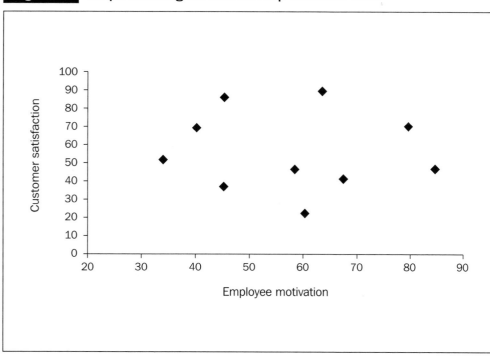

> One problem with a
> correlation is that it
> does not show cause
> and effect.

One problem with a correlation is that, although it describes the relationship between two sets of data, it does not show cause and effect.

In the example above, the senior management team may assume higher customer satisfaction is due in part to higher staff motivation but the statistic does not imply that. Both sets of data may be influenced by a third factor, for example the weather.

To determine likely causality, it is necessary to use a different approach, as described below.

Finding the drivers which impact most strongly on motivation

In this case the senior management team is interested in the main 'drivers' affecting an issue. In the context of this document the question would be 'what are the main drivers influencing motivation in our organisation?' or 'on what do we need to focus to influence motivation?'

This level of sophistication is not always necessary. Senior management teams often feel that they can spot the main drivers because they suspected what were in the first place, and the figures simply confirm their suspicions.

In order to answer the question using statistical methodology the data needs to be subjected to a causal analysis. At PricewaterhouseCoopers one management team decided to use this approach to help understand their data. In this example the question in the minds of senior management was:

What are the items which best predict success with our two strategic people initiatives:

- *to become the 'Employer of Choice', and*
- *establish 'A Clear Vision of the Future'?*

A statistical analysis of the causal relationship using the technique 'logistic regression' was carried out by Kevin Walker of the PricewaterhouseCoopers Survey Centre to identify the items.

'Employer of choice'

The statistical analysis identified five items which best predict, or 'drive', respondents' perception of PricewaterhouseCoopers' ability to achieve the 'employer of choice' strategy. Figure 7.11 is an 'opportunity map' showing the relationship between:

- each item's predictive strength (importance); and
- the score given by respondents for the top five items.

Items in the top two quadrants (high importance) typically get the highest priority for action planning.

Fig. 7.11 Opportunity map

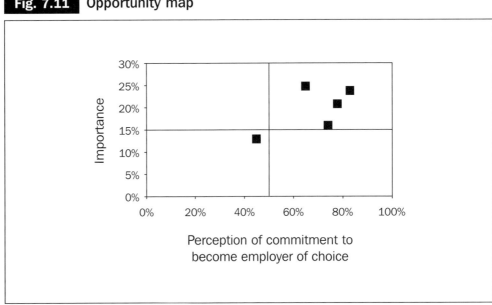

Perception of commitment to become employer of choice

The items were:

- 'Morale in my group is generally high.'
- 'In my group, we respect our clients' cultures in all the work we do.'
- 'My contributions are valued and appreciated.'

- 'I believe PwC invests in the long term.'
- 'Client opportunities are shared among partners in my group.'

In this case, possible conclusions would be to emphasise action which shows respect for client cultures, recognises consultant contributions, shares opportunities and demonstrates long-term investment.

'A clear vision of the future'

In a similar manner, the statistical analysis also identified five items which predict or 'drive' respondents' perception of PricewaterhouseCoopers' ability to achieve a 'clear vision' strategy (see Figure 7.12). The items were:

- 'We build long-term relationships with our clients.'
- 'Client opportunities are shared among partners in my group.'
- 'I am sufficiently informed about my group's plans.'
- 'We demonstrate real ability to work effectively with different cultures.'
- 'My performance reviews are conducted on a regular and timely basis.'

Here the priorities for action are less clear, but the senior management team established better information to help make their decisions on action to be taken.

Fig. 7.12 Opportunity map

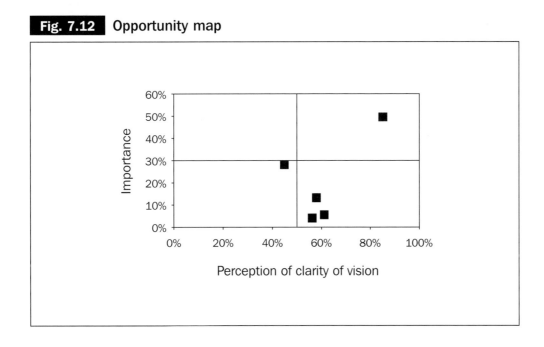

Finding a more revealing story by re-grouping questions

Here the senior management team would be looking for different groupings of items from those they initially used in their questionnaire.

For example a questionnaire may have been designed originally around organisational competencies such as levels of training, provision of pay and benefits, effectiveness of communications and management of resources.

By carrying out a statistical analysis (e.g. cluster analysis or factor analysis) which re-assembles items into groupings based on response patterns, a different story could emerge based on, for example, fairness of decision making, ability to learn from mistakes or lack of recognition.

Using professional advice

In all cases outlined above there are choices to be made about which statistics to use. The choices can be quite complex based on assumptions relating to the nature of your data. Consequently you should consult an experienced practitioner before taking action.

KEY POINT SUMMARY

- The simplest and least expensive way of searching for trends and themes is to 'eyeball' the data and use common sense.

- It is easier to eyeball the data if it has been arranged in rank order compared to internal 'best of class' with any large 'not sure' scores highlighted.

- It is becoming more common to compare data with external benchmarks and there are a number of benchmark clubs being established both by external agencies and organisations with common interests.

- Statistical techniques can be used to help identify whether differences are 'real' or due to chance.

- Statistical techniques can also be used to identify linear relationships (correlation) between sets of data but this approach does not indicate cause and effect.

- Statistical techniques are also available to show causal relationships (regression) between different sets of data.

- Statistical techniques are available to identify different groupings of your items and these new groupings could offer a different interpretation of your results (cluster or factor analysis).

- The main point about the use of statistics is make sure you choose the right one for the job. Ensure you use someone who is a formally trained practitioner.

Communicating results

This chapter requires the attention of the whole management team. If not carried out properly, the *communicating results* part of the exercise can result in a workforce less motivated than before the start of the survey. The following quote captures the point nicely:

> *Most people will put up with difficulties – it is part and parcel of organisational life. But few will put up with the same difficulties appearing year after year with no apparent attempt to resolve them.*
>
> Clive Newton, Senior Partner, PricewaterhouseCoopers.

Once people have completed a questionnaire they expect to see the results quickly. Traditionally this has been difficult because:

- two to three weeks could elapse between the first and last respondent returning their questionnaire;

- one to two weeks could elapse while hard copy questionnaires are input into the software manually;

- the data then has to be made meaningful and analysed, and trends/themes debated before a decision on what to do can be made;

- lastly, the data has to be simplified and printed, together with the conclusions and agreed action plan.

The process is summarised in Figure 8.1.

Fig. 8.1 Communicating results: timescale

Timescale	Process
2 weeks	Questionnaire completed
3 weeks	Questionnaire input
2 weeks	Data made meaningful
1 week	Trends and themes established
2 weeks	Actions planned
1 week	Data and action plans distributed

By the time all this has happened two months could have elapsed and everyone has either forgotten about the survey or become more cynical as to its outcome. Indeed some cynics would be right. It is not unknown for organisations to bin the results if they don't like or don't understand them.

This traditional approach can be reduced in length by overlapping some of the activities and separating out the trends and themes from the action plan – see Figure 8.2. Using this approach, for smaller organisations at least, it is possible to distribute the trends and themes within 3–4 weeks of the closing date for returns. That is an acceptable wait in the minds of most employees. However, using new technology it is becoming possible to cut down the time required to distribute the feedback even more significantly.

Fig. 8.2   Communicating results: reducing the timescale

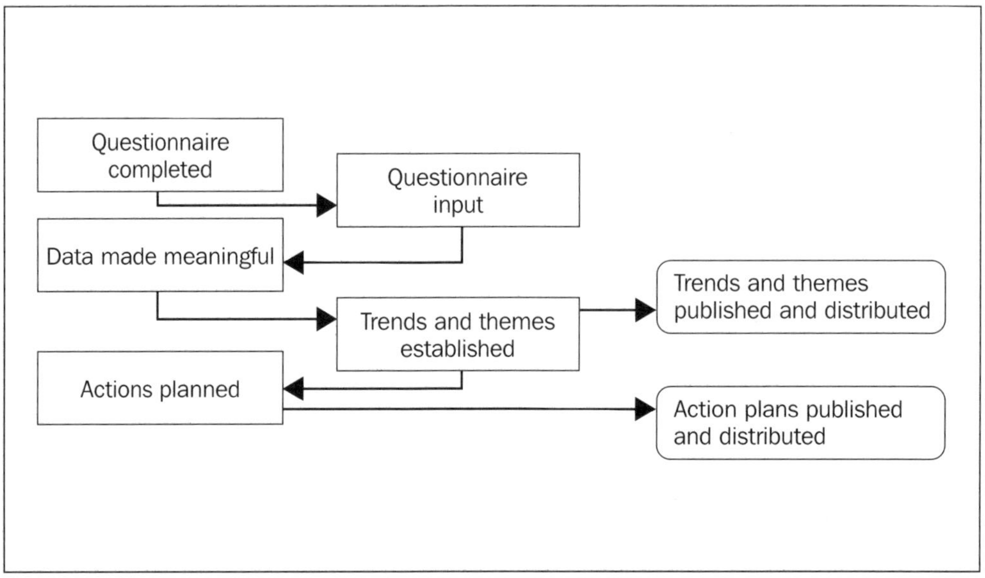

INITIAL DISTRIBUTION OF RESULTS

Separating out the survey results from the subsequent action plan can result in quicker feedback.

As the first people to see the results of a survey are normally the members of the senior management team, they often feel that they should immediately create an action plan as a response. While it is critical that the team should take action it is equally critical that people below the senior management team are involved too.

Separating out the survey results from the subsequent action plan can result in quicker feedback. Also it is also a good option to choose because it is then possible subsequently to involve everyone in discussing the priorities for improvement action. Here we look at how the four contributors distribute their results.

PricewaterhouseCoopers

At PricewaterhouseCoopers, the results are fed back to each business unit worldwide using their Lotus Notes system.

> *Feedback of results should be a routine event – just like financial results. The first time you receive them it takes a bit of time to work out what to do. But for the second and third times you can see what's changed and know what action to take.*
>
> Clive Newton, Senior Partner, PricewaterhouseCoopers.

Feedback is in the form of column charts which compare results of each business unit against suitable norms. (An example format, with dummy results and benchmarks, is given in Figure 8.3.) From there the business unit leaders are expected to cascade the results to their people. The way this is done depends on local circumstances.

Fig. 8.3   Example of PricewaterhouseCoopers' feedback format

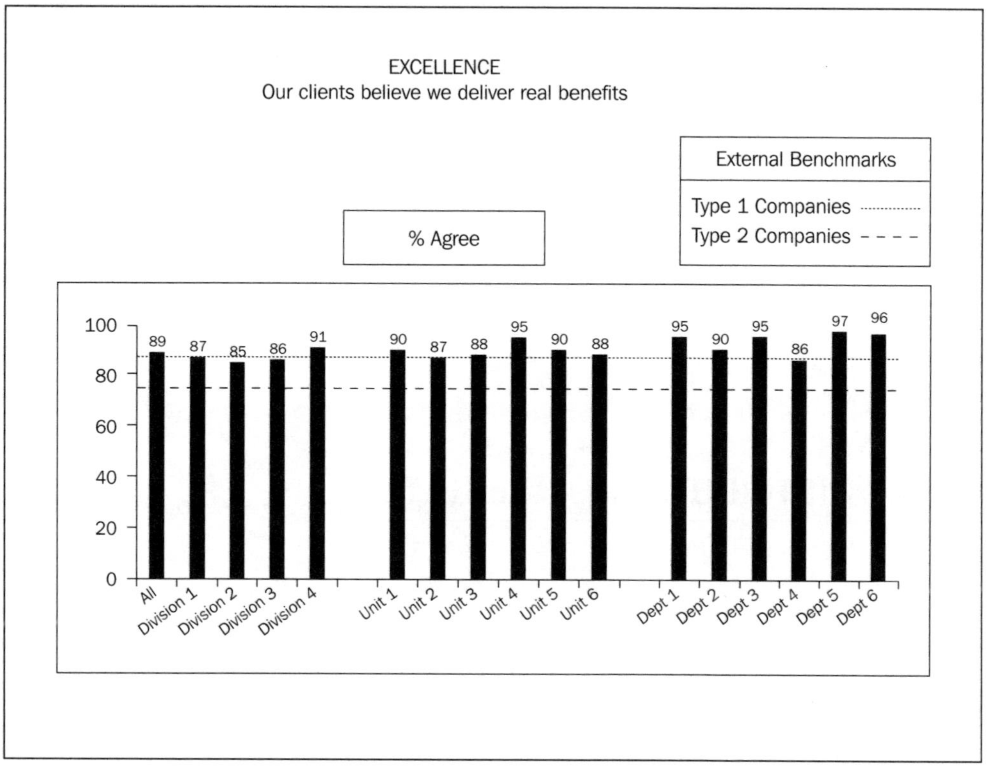

BT MNS&S

BT MNS&S used their web page to provide detailed feedback. Everyone received brief printed feedback, part of which is shown in Figure 8.4. Those employees requiring further information were referred to the website.

Fig. 8.4 Extract from BT MNS&S feedback

A Great Place to Work

What did you tell us?

Generally people do think that Multi-National Sales and Service is a 'good' place to work. We are getting it right in terms of:

- *Appreciation* – colleagues are supportive, contributions are valued, successes are celebrated within teams, professional knowledge and skills are highly valued.

- *Learning* – excellent customer relations, building long-term relationships and focusing on quality solutions.

- *Future focus* – we continually look for better ways of working, understand our customers' future needs, encourage innovative ideas within teams, and anticipate change.

- *Trust* – people feel trusted, respected and secure in support from their managers to take risks but improvements could be made by managers in giving honest feedback and empowering people.

- *Enjoyment* – people enjoy and get personal satisfaction from their job, they work in a friendly environment and morale is generally high, but people's quality of life and stress factors are areas for improvement.

While we are doing well in these areas we cannot be complacent – ours is a fast moving business and we need to do more to make MNS&S a 'great' place to work. Specifically we need to work on:

- *Collaboration* – in practice there are concerns about the willingness of other teams in MNS&S to share freely and support each other, relationships need to be more productive and people are not rewarded for cooperating with other teams.

- *Fairness* – improvements are needed in the consistent and fair treatment of people and how they are managed, and in enabling people to have a better balance between work and home life.

- *Simplicity* – greater changes and improvements are needed in simplifying the way we work by reducing bureaucracy, minimising duplication of effort, streamlining work practices and getting decision-making at a lower level.

A Great Place to Work webpage {LINK} contains full details of the initiative and the work that is going on. This is regularly updated with news and progress.

By using this approach they catered for the needs of two types of people – those who want a quick overview of the results and those who prefer to examine them in detail.

Airtours

Some Airtours Holidays staff do not have immediate access to e-mail or their intranet, so consequently their feedback is based on the printed form. In addition, managers invest a considerable amount of time briefing their people in groups. People are encouraged to become actively involved in action planning.

They take a significant amount of time and effort to make their feedback attractive and readable, with personal statements from both their managing director and director of human resources (see Figure 8.5).

People are encouraged to become actively involved in action planning.

Fig. 8.5 Airtours Holidays: feedback from the managing director

Shaping the way our business is run for the future

Your views, your feedback and your comments are vitally important to Airtours. They will play a strategic part in helping us to become the UK's preferred holiday company. That is the level of importance we place on your views.

This, the second Viewpoint Survey, shows that you believe we've made improvements in all areas of the business. And, overall, the results are 20 per cent better than the first survey.

That's good news. However, we recognise that not all of you feel that this is the case, and there are some areas on which we need to focus.

The booklet gives an overview of the key results compared with our last Viewpoint Survey, highlighting our biggest areas of improvement and where further work needs to be done.

You tell us we've got quality products, provide a quality service, you're proud to work for Airtours and you feel far more involved in the way the business is run.

But, despite an overall improvement, many of you feel that we can do better.

An example is communication where we improved by 13 per cent in the UK, but only 50 per cent of you believe that it's good.

You suggest we also need to look at teamwork, resources, planning and organising and career development.

Chris Mottershead – Managing Director, 1998, Airtours Holidays.

In designing their feedback document they judge that they have at least three types of interested parties. Some like to have a good read. Consequently part of the document is in typescript. Figure 8.6 gives an example.

Fig. 8.6 Airtours Holidays: feedback in words

Communication

Whilst we have improved, we still need to work harder on communication, especially in the UK. Our understanding of the information technology project is poor and this will be addressed. However, the majority of you feel you are well informed on the direction of Airtours, have regular meetings with your managers and know the company values.

Senior management need to communicate more effectively with you and provide more opportunities to have your say.

Some like to see at a glance what the results are, and to cater for this style Airtours used simple circles – the larger the circle the better the results (see Figure 8.7).

Fig. 8.7 Airtours Holidays: feedback at a glance

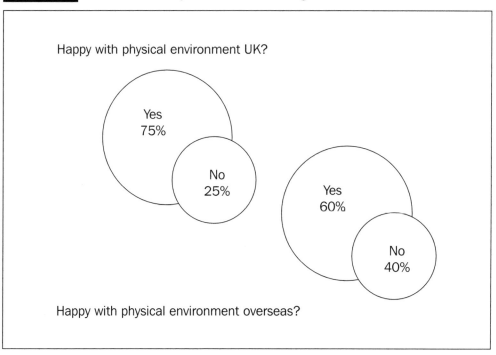

Elida Fabergé

The Elida Fabergé organisation-wide communication system makes use of video, so that the chairman's response to the survey results can be seen by all on locally based TVs. In the video the chairman makes it clear that he and his colleagues are presenting the overall 'headline' results and more detailed results available by site, function and department will be discussed in local team meetings.

The survey results are timed to link in with both company performance and plans for the future and consequently both survey and business results are included in the video. The structure of the video is as follows:

- explanation of how the results fit into company strategy;
- outline of overall company performance (growth, profitability, etc.);
- information on new product launches/relaunches;
- outline of specific factory performance (operating expenses, safety records, customer service, etc.);
- employee survey results:
  - comparison against the UK norm;
  - what people saw as being important to their work;
  - how satisfied people were with their work;
- board conclusion and business-wide action plan;
- employee involvement in local initiatives.

The feedback from Elida Fabergé is notable in that it links with the annual business cycle, provides all employees with a sense of how their company compares with other blue-chip UK businesses and highlights the interest of the chairman.

CASCADE TO INDIVIDUAL TEAMS

Once managers (and supervisors) have become familiar with the results and developed their own views on action needed, the organisation is ready to cascade to all remaining people.

In the case of PricewaterhouseCoopers the results are presented to interested parties in each business unit. They are given time to analyse them individually and are then divided into groups to discuss their observations. The 'break out' groups draw out their own themes and formulate possible action plans.

Subsequently their recommendations are debated by all participants and consensus on what the themes, priorities and actions to be taken is achieved. Figure 8.8 illustrates the approximate timing of this event.

Fig. 8.8 Structure of a PricewaterhouseCoopers business unit workshop

Timescale	Activity
9.00 – 9.15	Introduction and brief overview.
9.15 – 9.30	Fargus Global Survey Data.
9.30 – 10.00	Survey Centre Global Analysis.
10.00 – 10.45	Individually review the data. Participants extract key findings/issues and supporting data.
11.00 – 1.00	Break out groups to draw out themes and formulate possible actions.
2.00 – 3.00	Feedback recommendations to wider group with evidence.
3.00 – 4.00	Group to reach a consensus on what the priorities, themes and actions should be.

Yes, you take jumbo actions – these are important – but it is the hundreds of day-to-day actions that your managers and their people take which make the difference.

Clive Newton, Senior Partner, PricewaterhouseCoopers.

At Airtours teams are given the results relating to their area of operation as well as the 'all-organisation' scores. Their team is asked to discuss the results and draw conclusions about what action should be taken by the company and locally. Figure 8.9 shows a set of Airtours' guidelines on the holding of team briefings.

Fig. 8.9 Airtours Holidays' guidelines on team briefings

Airtours overseas cascade pack – guidelines for team briefings

Background

Opinion surveys help to identify areas for improvement so the surveys are in keeping with our strategy.

In addition, there are important messages about the Company strategy which need to be cascaded throughout the business.

Purpose of the cascade

To communicate the key results of the Viewpoint opinion survey and ensure that staff feel involved in action planning and implementation for future improvement areas.

Continued

Aims

To provide all staff with clarity on the main themes and results of the survey for the business and for overseas in particular

To outline where further improvements are needed

To contribute to the development of an overall Business Action Plan.

The cascade of Viewpoint

The cascade process consists of two activities:

- staff reading their own copy of the Viewpoint feedback booklet;
- a team cascade meeting and action planning session.

Preparation tips for the cascade process

Week one

Organise a venue which is suitable for getting your team together and where you can then split them into groups of 4–6 people.

Distribute the Viewpoint feedback booklet to your team.

Read and digest these notes and the Viewpoint booklet to ensure you are fully conversant with the data and the Action Planning process.

Week two

Hold your Cascade and Action Planning session.

The Cascade session will comprise the following stages:

- Introduction (5 mins)
- Feedback – Company Results (15 mins)
- Feedback – Overseas Results (10 mins)
- Action Planning (25 mins)
- Prioritising Ideas (5 mins)
- Summary and Close (5 mins)

Week three

Return your manager's summary pro forma to the Director of Overseas Operations and the Cascade audit process form to Personnel or Human Resources.

> If carried out properly the cascade system can be incredibly energising for an organisation.

If carried out properly the cascade system can be incredibly energising for an organisation. People feel that their voice has been heard and they are being involved in suggesting improvement action.

There is a cost of course in that you need to release people from their work. But usually the benefits derived from such a move are judged to outweigh the costs.

KEY POINT SUMMARY

- Results should be quickly distributed throughout your organisation. It is usually quicker to separate out the results from the subsequent action plan and distribute the plan at a later date.

- When creating feedback, think about the different types of people who will receive it and design the feedback to be meaningful to them.

- Once managers have had a chance to assimilate the results they should discuss them with their team and identify their own priorities for action.

- There is a cost involved in doing this – that of your people's time – but this is usually outweighed by the improvement action generated.

Implementing improvement action

9

117

This chapter should be read by the full senior management team.

The measuring instrument has now enabled informed discussion about those business issues that people have felt in need of attention. It is time to take action.

DECIDING WHAT ACTIONS TO TAKE

Typically improvement action can be categorised as follows:

- organisation-wide initiatives;
- functionally based initiatives;
- process improvements;
- individual action.

In making decisions on priorities, take the following into consideration:

- Initially, take action which has high impact and quick results.
- Take action only after costs and benefits have been established.
- Some action will need associated training and this is expanded on below.
- A way of logging progress should be established to prevent duplication of effort, to enable subsequent updates to be communicated, and to recognise effort and success.

> The measuring instrument has now enabled informed discussion about those business issues that people have felt in need of attention.

FACILITATING ACTION THROUGH TRAINING

Often the results of the survey indicate that a range of training is required, management, non-management or both. In terms of improving motivation, management training and development often focus on the need for a more participatative or supportive style while the equivalent non-management training is aimed at encouraging involvement through development of knowledge, skills and attitude.

The use of management training/development

At PricewaterhouseCoopers MCS they have developed a Supportive Leadership Initiative for all partners. This involves each partner assessing him or herself against the profile of critical competencies:

- developing client relationships;
- learning and coaching;
- operating globally;

- seizing opportunities;

- sharing.

Gaps in skills/knowledge are identified by self-assessment and initiate development action, including personal coaching where appropriate. The results of the development action are measured using a process of upward feedback. Additionally all experienced consultants have been offered a coach development course which is supported by web-based information and advice.

Lastly, PricewaterhouseCoopers revalued their training programmes by:

- making it a serious 'offence' to cancel at short notice;

- considering only consultants willing and able to act as tutors on courses for promotion to partner;

- expecting partners to tutor on courses for at least five days per year.

Specific training in motivational skills

One major training intervention initiated by an international oil company is another example of the use of training to change management style and hence impact on motivation. All managers are required to attend a three-day workshop designed to explore the issues of people management and how management behaviour can significantly affect employee motivation and, subsequently, results. The course encourages participants to visualise themselves working in seven roles: organiser, problem-solver, communicator, anticipator, developer, motivator and producer (see Figure 9.1).

Fig. 9.1 The seven roles of the manager

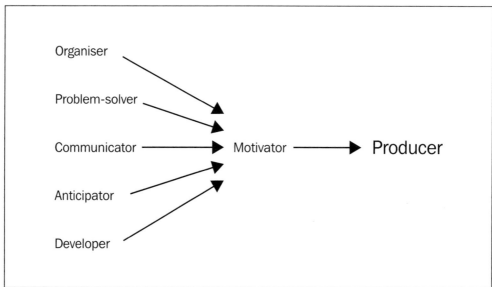

The first five roles all impact on the motivation of team members which then drives the production of results.

- *The manager as an organiser* emphasises the need to set a good example through self-organisation and then to ensure that the energies of the team are maximised through well defined work values and business practices.

- *The manager as a problem-solver* debates when and how to involve team members, emphasising that this should not happen all the time and that involvement does not include abdication of responsibility. The module develops the skills for using standard participative problem-solving techniques (brainstorming, pareto, cause–effect analysis, decision matrix, etc.).

- *The manager as a communicator* investigates how often different types of information should be transmitted to team members and discusses how a manager's personal style can get in the way of – or facilitate – good two-way communication. It also looks at the ways of reducing misunderstandings occurring while working in an international and/or multicultural environment.

- *The manager as an anticipator* emphasises the role of helping the team to understand what influences are causing change and ensuring the team members are capable of responding to them. The module also looks at the role of the team members in generating improvements to the way they do things.

- *The manager as a developer* looks at the personal style of the team leader both in the terms of self-development and developing team members through coaching, training and the choice of suitable objectives.

- *The manager as a motivator* summarises how the previous roles can influence the motivation of team members by impacting on their various personal needs (see Chapter 2).

- The workshop finishes with *the manager as a producer*, emphasising the difference between the 'activator' role and the 'producer' role, and discusses the use of objective-setting, delegation and choice of team measurements.

Non-management training and development

At BT MNS&S their survey identified a need to emphasise the importance of a learning environment within their non-management population as well as their managers. A Learning Fund was set up, which offered up to £350 per person to take part in a wide range of learning activities. Individuals were responsible for identifying the type of course they wanted to carry out themselves. Examples of the learning carried out ranged from driving lessons to information technology courses and GCSEs.

At Elida Fabergé 'personal growth' was one of the issues identified by their board as meriting company-wide attention. The managers already had a strong performance development planning process (PDP) and this is being extended to cover all employees. Agreed personal development plans are created through discussion between each individual and their line manager and implementation of these plans is then monitored.

ACTIONS TAKEN BY CONTRIBUTORS

Actions taken by contributors link well with those influences in motivation outlined in Chapter 2.

Senior management behaviour

As well as offering training to managers and non-managers alike, there is a trend towards explicitly defining values and then measuring how well managers are living up to them.

At Airtours they have initiated actions to impact on their people's behaviour in general and the behaviour of management in particular. The senior management team has instigated a major programme to define and emphasise the Airtours Holidays values. Staff were asked about what values Airtours currently had and what they would like to see. This would potentially create the most effective working culture for their people and ultimately was seen as a way to maximise business performance.

The results have been integrated into all aspects of business life (see Figure 9.2) and has impacted on the structure of their Viewpoint survey, the content of 360° feedback and their performance management process.

All senior managers participate in the Airtours 360° feedback process, which includes discussion of how they 'live' the values with their boss. This approach is being cascaded to all managers, with heads of department discussing the results.

PricewaterhouseCoopers too have established an upward feedback system designed to give anyone who manages others feedback on their impact as leaders. The feedback is based around the PricewaterhouseCoopers value set, the framework of which is shown in Figure 9.3.

Fig. 9.2 Airtours Holidays' value set

Airtours Holidays values

Organised and professional

■ Planning and prioritising

■ Delivering consistent quality products and services

■ Working as an effective team

■ Communicating clearly, consistently and effectively

■ Demonstrating clarity of vision goals and objectives.

Creative and inspiring

■ Challenging what we do and finding better ways to do things

■ Encouraging, listening and building on ideas

■ Setting a positive example

■ Seizing opportunities to learn, coach and motivate

■ Searching for opportunities for innovation.

Friendly and enthusiastic

■ Sharing and celebrating success

■ Making people feel special

■ Demonstrating energy and drive

■ Giving the extra mile

■ Smiling and having fun.

Genuine and trustworthy

■ Delivering what we promise

■ Respecting our customers, colleagues and suppliers

■ Taking responsibility for our actions

■ Acknowledging mistakes, putting them right and learning from them

■ Showing understanding and concern.

| Fig. 9.3 | PricewaterhouseCoopers' value set |

Excellence

- Delivering what we promise
- Developing creative solutions
- Developing knowledge and expertise
- Being alert to change and moving fast

Teamwork

- Delivering best solutions through working together
- Building productive long-term relationships
- Showing respect for the individual
- Sharing knowledge, experience, resources and opportunities

Leadership

- Inspiring people to deliver the best
- Seizing the initiative and welcoming responsibility
- Having a clear sense of where we want to go
- Sharing high standards of ethical behaviour and professionalism

Improving how people are managed

At Airtours two early issues which emerged from their survey were, firstly, the view that people were not recognised for their loyalty to the company, and, secondly, people felt the need to be more involved. In response, they introduced two initiatives:

People were not recognised for their loyalty to the company, and, people felt the need to be more involved.

- a long service recognition scheme;
- 'Open Forum'.

Airtours introduced a long service recognition scheme which involves the managing director and the board hosting a champagne reception and presenting Long Service Certificates. Staff also receive gifts from the boss on their 10th, 15th, 20th, and 25th anniversary with the company. The celebrations are well reported in their magazine as shown in the box below.

> **Extract from the Airtours magazine:**
>
> A further Long Service Awards Reception was held in January. Those members of staff who have had a Long Service Anniversary were invited to join members of the board for a champagne reception. Certificates were presented and pictures taken as a memento for all those who attended. The reception provided another opportunity to recognise the valuable contribution our long serving colleagues have made.

The development of the Airtours 'Open Forum' is a good example of how the company has improved two-way communication and involvement as a result of feedback from the Viewpoint '97 Survey.

The survey highlighted the fact that people felt that big improvements could be made to two-way communication and people's feeling of involvement in the business. As part of the Action Plan, the idea of an employee discussion forum developed. This was not immediately implemented – discussion groups were organised to sound out people's opinions and external benchmarks were sought from Tesco, Going Places and the BBC.

The end result is the Airtours Holidays 'Open Forum', a regular two-way information flow about Airtours Holidays business issues and a process of raising and resolving issues of concern to employees. Extracts from the published information leaflet are given in Figure 9.4.

Fig. 9.4 Extracts from information leaflet on Airtours Holidays 'Open Forum'

Airtours open forum

Why have a forum?

■ You told us you want to be listened to and consulted more (through Viewpoint)

■ You want simple, clear and concise lines of communication

What is a forum?

■ A two-way communication and information flow about business issues

■ A process for raising and resolving issues that concern you

What the forum will not be

■ A way to raise personal grievances

■ A way to negotiate terms and conditions

Continued

What's in it for you?

■ Regular ongoing process to act on issues

■ A listening, consulting opportunity

■ A chance to voice your own and your colleagues' opinions and ideas

Who will be involved?

■ Elected representatives from UK and overseas

■ Our MD and members of the Board

■ Internal Communications Manager

■ Our Director of HR

How will it work?

■ Meetings will be held twice a year

■ Agenda items can be given to your area representative

■ Updates before and after the meetings will be available in *The Happening* (company magazine), from your representative and at your team briefing

■ If you want to be a representative you can nominate yourself as long as you are supported by a colleague

■ Alternatively you can nominate and support a colleague

The role of the representative

■ To gather agenda items from colleagues in your area

■ To attend and input to the forum meetings

■ To be committed to the role and your colleagues, even if their views are ones you may not always agree with

■ To update your colleagues on outcomes and action points

■ To complete the representatives' training course

■ To work with other forum attendees as a team

The Airtours survey also identified that many people below management levels did not fully understand how their work activities linked to the annual business plan. In response to this feedback they introduced balanced business scorecards as part of their management process.

The scorecard has the aim of harnessing interests and abilities to meet organisational goals. The activities included in the process are:

■ a cascade of objectives, starting with the annual business planning process and ending with the agreement of personal objectives. This is designed to ensure all people play a part in supporting the objectives of the company;

- regular reviews and feedback to support the achievement of objectives;

- coaching both collectively and individually in order to enhance the performance and learning ability of team members;

- a personal development plan which sets out the development needs of an individual, incorporating a wide range of development activities.

They see the system as a continuous process designed to ensure that, through learning, development and personal growth, an individual's performance contributes to company goals.

At BT MNS&S their survey helped identify a priority relating to the perception of fairness through equal opportunities. They consequently invested in raising managerial awareness and understanding of diversity issues in order to help people feel valued for their individual skills and experience.

Also, they augmented their approach to recognition for effort and success by including the whole family. Spouses and children have to put up with a lot of disruption in today's unpredictable business environment. They held a day out at Alton Towers for the whole directorate where the employees, together with their families, could relax and enjoy themselves.

At Elida Fabergé they identified better recognition and better work–life balance as two themes on which to base their improvement activities. In order to recognise effort and success they introduced 'thank you' cards and £15 retail vouchers, and a Recognition Champion was appointed to promote and monitor the scheme. The following quote shows what results were achieved:

> *It has been a brilliant year for recognition. Thank you cards have been very popular with around 1000 being despatched this year. There has, too, been a fantastic response to the retail vouchers with over 400 people nominated.*
>
> *Elida Fabergé, 1999*

In order to address the work–life balance issue they initiated two organisational projects and encouraged local improvement action. The two projects focused firstly on what people could stop doing and secondly how work could be tackled more effectively. Local initiatives included the introduction of flexible working hours, increased working from home and part-time working.

PricewaterhouseCoopers also found work–life balance to be a major issue. Many consultants felt that the pressures of travel and staying way from home had become too great to handle.

The business was tasked with finding solutions to this problem. One business unit in the United States came up with the concept of '5–4–3'. This policy means that consultants work five days on their client work, and therefore are able to charge for the five days, but only four days are spent on the client site. The fifth

Pricewaterhouse-Coopers also found work–life balance to be a major issue.

127

day is spent at the consultant's home or office and means that only three nights away from home are involved.

This policy has proved such a significant success that it has now been adopted on all assignments across business units worldwide. The consultant spends less time away from home, and the client has a greater chance of consultant continuity through significantly reduced 'churn'. Some clients have even introduced the same policy for their own staff.

The PricewaterhouseCoopers surveys have also helped to focus on remuneration. As a partnership with regulatory and independence restrictions, they are not able to offer formal share options and consultants who could not participate in the partner bonuses felt disadvantaged. This consequently had an impact on consultant retention. In the United States the solution they opted for has been to create a Consultant Share Unit. These are allocated to consultants on the basis of their performance, and their value is based on the partnership performance.

This has been very successful and has now been rolled out across Asia Pacific and is being reviewed in Europe.

Changes to the physical environment can send a powerful signal that 'management are listening'.

Improving how resources are managed

At Airtours one area of feedback confirmed by their Viewpoint '97 survey was that some people were dissatisfied with the environment in the head office building. In order to tackle this head office problem, Airtours opted against the use of focus groups and decided to commission a specialist environmental survey. This covered:

■ the office equipment;

■ workstation design;

■ first aid, medical and safety provisions;

■ car parking facilities;

■ toilet facilities;

■ canteen facilities.

The issues were all 'satisfiers' in the sense that an environment perceived to be below expected standard causes irritation and complaint, while one at the expected standard does not generally increase motivation levels other than for a short time. On the other hand, changes to 'the environment' can have a low cost/high impact value and help to demonstrate that management are willing to take action as a result of the survey.

One of the actions that Airtours took was to refurbish their head office canteen completely over one weekend. Apart from the benefits of an improved canteen, this sent a powerful signal that 'management are listening'. Other responses included:

■ reducing glare from visual display units;

- developing and stocking a first aid room;
- practising fire evacuation procedures;
- making benches and picnic tables available;
- negotiating membership of the local sports club;
- providing smoking facilities.

At PricewaterhouseCoopers MCS, as a result of one of their earlier surveys, a major opportunity to improve consultant effectiveness was confirmed. Responses to items on the use of technology suggested that the firm was not making best use of information technology. As a result all consultants without access to a PC were issued with laptops and associated software. More recent surveys have begun to refocus attention towards improving help desk support.

Improving systems and procedures

At BT MNS&S their 'Great Place to Work' survey identified the need for better collaboration within and across different sectors. A major knowledge management programme was already underway and feedback from the survey fed into this programme.

> *There are concerns about the willingness of other teams to share freely and support each other – relationships need to be more productive.*

A knowledge interchange network was developed which provided all people in BT MNS&S with easy access to information technology that helped them to share and build on ideas and knowledge.

Another issue identified was the need for greater simplicity in the way they work.

> *Improvements are needed in simplifying the way we work by reducing bureaucracy, minimising duplication of effort, streamlining work practices and devolving decision-making to a lower level.*

An example of action they took as a result was to reduce the sources of information people needed to travel overseas. They created a Globetrotters Guide which pulled together useful websites for the traveller.

At PricewaterhouseCoopers MCS their post-merger survey highlighted the need to create worldwide business management processes. These were designed to coordinate with the PricewaterhouseCoopers values and cover:

- *Client Services*, including bid and risk management, client relationship management, business methodology and sales activity management;

- *People and Knowledge*, including attracting, deploying, developing and retaining;

- *Business Management*, including investment management and financial management.

Apart from making the organisation as a whole more efficient, the existence of a common way of doing things worldwide facilitates the movement of consultants from one country to another and one assignment to another.

Improving reputation

At Airtours their Viewpoint '95 survey helped to confirm two issues relating to image which their people felt strongly about. The responses showed that:

- travel agents had insufficient detailed knowledge of the company's products and services;

- customers were receiving new product information before the staff.

Airtours has worked hard to rectify these.

In the case of travel agents, Airtours has not only restructured its sales team but also expanded it significantly to ensure that all agents have closer contact with a specific manager. The manager is responsible for ensuring that agents are fully briefed on both new and existing products.

In addition, the holiday company has increased the number of educational visits aimed at ensuring counter staff and branch managers have personal experience of the main holiday destinations.

And, in order to ensure staff are aware of new products as quickly as possible, product features are included in their company magazine, *The Happening*, as well as via video and internal press releases.

KEY POINT SUMMARY

- Once the talking is finished, action must be taken.

- The action chosen should, initially, be of high impact and show quick results.

- Decisions as to what actions to take should be subjected to standard cost-benefit analysis.

- Associated training for both management and non-management is sometimes necessary to facilitate the implementation of improvement action.

- Actions taken by contributors impact on the key influences on motivation outlined in Chapter 2.

Taking stock and recognising success

This last chapter should be read by the full senior management team.

Not only should action be taken, but it should be seen to be taken. By publishing progress people are encouraged to retain the link between their 'voice at the table' and subsequent action. It is this link which is a key to improving morale and motivation – without it the value of most of the work described in previous chapters is significantly diminished.

> Not only should action be taken, but it should be seen to be taken.

AIRTOURS

At Airtours their progress is reported bi-monthly in their magazine called *The Happening*. Figure 10.1 is an example of one of their earlier publications.

Fig. 10.1 Extract from Airtours Holidays' magazine *The Happening*

Airtours Holidays – update

We will be reporting on how the Viewpoint Survey Action Plan is coming along in the next edition of *The Happening*. It is important that everyone knows about the progress being made and how they can find out more about Viewpoint especially as the Action Plan was put together from ideas staff put forward!

Here's some highlights from what's been happening around the business over the last couple of months:

Long service

Long Service events will now be held twice a year. The next event is due to take place towards the end of July.

Knowledge of other parts of the business

Profiles of different departments/resorts will appear in each addition of *The Happening*. In the last edition Menorca was profiled and in this edition you will find a profile of Staff Travel. These profiles will continue so let us know if there's a department you'd like to know more about!

Communication and involvement

We are looking to develop a discussion forum, where employees will have the chance to question senior managers about the big issues affecting the business and to give their own points of view.

The Internal Communications team has been working to put together proposals for a team briefing process.

The publication *The Happening* – itself the result of a need identified by Viewpoint '97 – is well read by at least some staff judging by the 'tailback' comments:

> *What a great mixture of small and large project updates in the last edition. Good focus and very professional.*
>
> *Everyone I speak to loves the Viewpoint survey updates. If any page was to be kept, keep this one.*

BT MNS&S

At BT MNS & S they also issued progress reports. Figure 10.2 provides an outline of one report.

Fig. 10.2 Outline of a BT MNS & S progress report

A great place to work

So what are we doing?

The key behaviour that we need to develop and recognise is *collaborative working within and across sectors*.

- Knowledge management techniques and technology are being implemented across the Division to support this.

- A knowledge of interchange network is being developed.

For collaborative working to flourish and develop it needs an atmosphere of *continual learning* and *valuing others*.

- Sales Skills Transformation programme is being developed.

- Learning Fund has been launched. To date 50% of non-managers have requested funds.

To get the best contribution and cooperation from people and a willingness to share their ideas and be open to those of others', you have to understand and *value differences that people have*.

- Diversity Awareness Workshops – all people managers will be invited to attend a workshop.

From the survey *simplification of processes and systems* and making it easier for people to do their jobs is the main area that needs improving.

- Globetrotters Guide – one-stop showing of information for people to do their jobs is the main area that needs improving.

We are also reviewing the people systems and processes to ensure that they are not overcomplicated and that they recognise, reward and reinforce the behaviours of 'A Great Place to Work'.

ELIDA FABERGÉ

At Elida Fabergé, as well as reporting on progress to staff, they take steps to coordinate their departmental actions, with each manager being required regularly to report on the progress of his or her improvements.

There are two good reasons for doing this. Firstly, the number of formally registered improvement actions can be used as a hard measure of employee motivation. Secondly, it is easier to celebrate success and recognise teams for what they are doing – a motivator in itself.

Figure 10.3 contains an extract from an organisation report. Each department has established its own priority issues and improvement actions. Each action has a simple status report linked to it and progress is monitored monthly or quarterly.

Fig. 10.3 Extract from an Elida Fabergé organisation report

Department	Priority issues/Actions	Status
Human Resources	■ Personal development ■ Workload ■ Interface with other sites ■ Recognition	■ Personal Development Plans completed ■ New HR administrator ■ Visits to sites for new staff ■ Regular Dept programmes
House Services	■ Work–life balance ■ Recognition ■ Personal growth	■ Leave at 5.00 pm, limit weekend working ■ Increased use of 'thank you' system ■ All job descriptions reviewed
Business Systems	■ Career counselling ■ Internal communication ■ Team building across sites	■ All started, head of department to review quarterly
Commercial	■ Pay ■ Reaction to survey ■ Workload	■ Salary benchmark survey cascaded ■ Regular reviews in place ■ Range of actions in hand
Logistics	■ Training and development ■ Resources ■ Impact on society	■ Personal Development Plans ongoing ■ Replacement contractors, in hand ■ Policy and actions communicated

Continued

Field Sales	■ Personal growth ■ Communication ■ Recognition ■ Home/work life	■ New training programme and individual schedules ■ New team meeting structure ■ New achievement award: annual social event ■ Better options for working from home
Market Research	■ Feedback customer comments to team ■ Workload ■ Advancement ■ Communication	■ Ongoing at team meetings ■ Additional resource in place ■ New structure in place ■ System of team meetings and awaydays in place
Marketing Communication	■ Work/personal life balance ■ Fair pay/benefits ■ Improved priority setting	■ Part-time working introduced ■ Salary adjustment made ■ Regular status meetings

KEY POINT SUMMARY

■ Without this part of the process the value of previous actions is significantly diminished.

■ Improvement action should be regularly monitored and people offered regular updates on progress.

■ Monitoring should be by short departmental or project reports on progress to the senior management team.

■ Updates should be provided to all, using regular communication channels.

Conclusion

Are the benefits of investing all this time and effort worth the cost? Let us have a look at the benefits which have been mentioned earlier. If you approach your survey seriously here are some likely results:

Benefits to employees

After initial suspicion, employees normally welcome questionnaires (as long as they are not overwhelmed by them). They see that the aggregation of their responses provides a 'voice at the table' which is taken seriously and contributes to policy and strategy.

When improvements are made, and as long as they are linked to the survey results, they enhance both morale and motivation.

Benefits to the senior management team

Communication channels between senior managers and employees become clearer. The senior management team can reasonably assert that they know what their people are thinking. They establish valid and reliable feedback on how people think and feel about the way the organisation is managed.

Benefits to managers

Managers can see how they are doing compared to the organisation norm, particularly in relation to people management skills, and can take informed steps to improve the way they manage.

Benefits to the bottom line

By implementing improvements the bottom line can be enhanced as a result of reduced costs and increased sales. The increased sales are particularly relevant when customer-facing staff are energised.

And finally

We will leave it to an anonymous respondent to one of the Pricewaterhouse-Coopers surveys to finish this book. He or she chose a form of words on which the author cannot improve:

The survey is a good idea. Well done for trying it. It will establish itself if two tests are met:

1 You publish the results and are seen to act on them.

2 You run another one in the not too distant future which, in its content, shows that you have learned and acted on this one.

However, surveys are only one way of addressing the inevitable human organisation issue of how to encourage and enable the speaking of truth. Good luck in creating the rest.

Anonymous.

Motivators and satisfiers

Here are some examples of items you could use in your own questionnaire. *You should amend the wording to suit your circumstances, replacing (my organisation) with the name of your organisation. If you want to use the FCP comparative database, do not change the meaning.*

	Motivators	Satisfiers
Senior management behaviour	Leaders in (*my organisation*) stimulate people to do their best In (*my organisation*) quality of output is seen as all-important	Leaders in (*my organisation*) can implement major change successfully
How people are managed	I know how my work contributes to organisational goals My work regularly gives me a sense of personal achievement My work regularly allows me to use my know-how My manager takes an active interest in me as an individual I feel involved in decisions that affect my work I have enough opportunity to keep my know-how up to date Innovative ideas are encouraged in my team I can see a relationship between effort and reward	Decisions made about people in (*my organisation*) are normally fair The right people are appointed into the right jobs I am satisfied with health and safety arrangements in my workplace I am satisfied with my physical working conditions (temperature, lighting, etc.) I am satisfied with my current benefits package My pay is fair compared to people doing similar work
Management of resources		I normally have enough information I need to do my job well I normally have the necessary equipment and supplies to do my job well Current staffing levels are about right to enable the expected quality of output
Decisions taken	Decision making is made at the lowest possible level	
Processes		We have well organised systems and procedures
Turf wars		Departments co-operate to get the job done
Investing in the future	(*My organisation*) invests for the future	
Reputation and success	(*My organisation*) is successful I am proud to be associated with (*my organisation*)	(*My organisation*) takes environmental issues seriously

In order to receive comparative data, send your results to FCP at the address given at the front of the book